HOW THE EBOOKS WORK

The eBooks are provided in EPUB file format. Please note that you will need an eBook reader installed on your device to open the file. Many devices come with this as standard, but you may still need to install one manually from Google Play.

The eBook content is identical to the content in the printed guide.

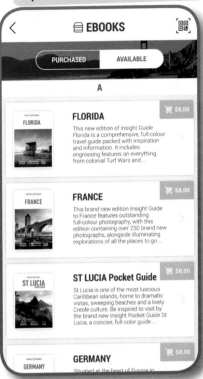

HOW TO DOWNLOAD THE WALKING EYE APP

1. Download the Walking Eye App from the App Store or Google Play.
2. Open the app and select the scanning function from the main menu.
3. Scan the QR code on this page – you will then be asked a security question to verify ownership of the book.
4. Once this has been verified, you will see your eBook in the purchased ebook section, where you will be able to download it.

Other destination apps and eBooks are available for purchase separately or are free with the purchase of the Insight Guide book.

INSIGHT ⦿ GUIDES

EXPLORE

AMSTERDAM

⦿ Walking Eye App

YOUR FREE EBOOK AVAILABLE THROUGH THE WALKING EYE APP

Your guide now includes a free eBook to your chosen destination,
for the same great price as before. Simply download the Walking Eye
App from the App Store or Google Play to access your free eBook.

HOW THE WALKING EYE APP WORKS

Through the Walking Eye App, you can purchase a range of eBooks and destination
content. However, when you buy this book, you can download the corresponding
eBook for free. Just see below in the grey panel where to find your free content and
then scan the QR code at the bottom of this page.

Destinations: Download essential destination content featuring recommended sights and attractions, restaurants, hotels and an A–Z of practical information, all available for purchase.

Ships: Interested in ship reviews? Find independent reviews of river and ocean ships in this section, all available for purchase.

eBooks: You can download your free accompanying digital version of this guide here. You will also find a whole range of other eBooks, all available for purchase.

Free access to travel-related blog articles about different destinations, updated on a daily basis.

CONTENTS

Introduction
Recommended Routes for…   6
Explore Amsterdam   10
Food and Drink   16
Shopping   20
History: Key Dates   22

Directory
Accommodation   92
Restaurants   100
Nightlife   108
A–Z   110
Books and Film   122

Credits
About This Book   124
Credits   125
Index   126

Best Routes
1. The Golden Age Canals   26
2. The Principal Squares   32
3. The Museum Quarter   37
4. The Old Centre (The Wallen)   43
5. The Zoo District   46
6. The Harbour   49
7. The Canals by Pedal Bike   52
8. Amsterdam by Tram   54
9. By Bicycle along the River Amstel 57
10. The Jordaan   60
11. The Jewish Quarter   63
12. Amsterdamse Bos   66
13. Leidseplein   69
14. Rembrandtplein   72
15. Red-Light District   75
16. Haarlem and Zandvoort   78
17. The IJsselmeer by Bike   83
18. The Hague   86

ART LOVERS

With three outstanding art museums (the Van Gogh, the Stedelijk and the Rijksmuseum), Amsterdam's Museum Quarter (route 3) matches any in the world, while Rembrandt's House can be found in the Jewish Quarter (route 11).

RECOMMENDED ROUTES FOR...

ESCAPING THE CROWDS

It's easy to escape the city by taking a bike north along the coast (route 17) across what used to be the Zuiderzee, or heading south to the wooded park, the Amsterdamse Bos (route 12).

FAMILIES

See the zoo and the Tropenmuseum Junior in the Zoo District (route 5), or the NEMO Science Centre and the Maritime Museum around the harbour (route 6).

HISTORY BUFFS

The Old Centre (route 4) includes the old Stock Exchange and Oude Kerk, while the canals of the 16th- and 17th-century Golden Age can be strolled along on route 1.

MUSIC LOVERS

Lovers of classical music should check the concerts on at the Concertgebouw (route 3), while rock fans will want to see who's playing at the Melkweg, one of the city's top music clubs (route 13).

NIGHT OWLS

The Leidseplein (route 13) and Rembrandtplein (route 14) offers bars and nightclubs galore, while the Red-Light District provides other entertainment for the broad-minded (route 15).

RAINY DAYS

When you have Amsterdam's wonderful Museum Quarter (route 3) you can escape the rain for hours, while another option is to go exploring Amsterdam by tram: see the sights and stay dry (route 8).

SEASIDE FUN

Head to The Hague (route 18) and its neighbouring seaside resort of Scheveningen, or the brasher resort of Zandvoort near Haarlem (route 16), both easily reached from Amsterdam.

INTRODUCTION

An introduction to Amsterdam's geography, customs and culture, plus illuminating background information on cuisine, history and what to do when you're there.

Explore Amsterdam   10

Food and Drink   16

Shopping   20

History: Key Dates   22

EXPLORE AMSTERDAM

Amsterdam is one of the friendliest and most romantic cities in Europe. Its canals delight, its museums impress, yet it's also an edgy city known for its liberal views. It is, in short, a city like no other.

Amsterdam grew out of nothing, turning from a tiny fishing village to the heart of the Dutch Empire. Its Dutch East Indian influences in particular are still evident, from grand buildings constructed during that era to a sizeable Indonesian population whose food is a tantalisingly spicy contrast to the more solid Dutch dishes.

Water is central to Amsterdam's history, geography and culture. The fishermen who first built their huts at the mouth of the River Amstel at the beginning of the 13th century earned a good living from the fertile fishing grounds of the Zuiderzee, although they and their families were at the mercy of wind and sea in that low-lying, swampy delta. Yet the community flourished, particularly once a dam was built to hold the Zuiderzee at bay. A by-product of this Amstel dam was the creation of a good anchorage, at the point where the Centraal Station now stands.

Yet for all its rich history, Amsterdam is very much a 21st-century city, famed for its tolerant attitudes to sex and drugs in particular – tolerant but never unconcerned, and the city's laws and attitudes do change. What doesn't change is its appeal to visitors, who flock there from all over the world.

GEOGRAPHY

With a population of over 850,000, Amsterdam is the Netherlands' biggest city, and its capital, though the seat of government is nearby in The Hague (see route 18). It's located in the Netherlands province of North Holland, and the country is often referred to as Holland although The Kingdom of the Netherlands is the full correct name.

A large part of Amsterdam's charm lies in its network of canals. The *grachtengordel*, the horseshoe of concentric canals that encloses the city centre, is the city's most timeless area. Names such as Prinsengracht (Princes' Canal), Herengracht (Gentlemen's Canal) and Keizersgracht (Emperor's Canal) are redolent of Amsterdam's Golden Age elegance.

From a visitor's point of view it means you're never far away from a delightful canal view. It also means parts of the city are not easy to navigate by car, making it somewhere best-explored on foot. The main dan-

The Blauwbrug and the River Amstel.

ger is in stepping out in front of a bicycle, the city's most popular form of transport. There's also a good public transport system (see page 119), though it's used much more by locals than by visitors as walking is so easy – and easy on the eye.

HISTORY

Originally named Aemstelledamme, that little fishing settlement soon expanded to become a commodities market, to which influxes of Flemish weavers and Jewish merchants made considerable contributions. In 1275 – the year in which the city was officially founded – Count Floris V granted the people of Aemstelledamme toll-free passage on the waterways. This development encouraged further growth in trade. Ships unloaded cargoes of Baltic timber, salt and spices on what is now the Dam, and sailed away laden with cloth, furnishings and grain.

The Golden Age

Amsterdam's Golden Age began towards the end of the 16th century. The city experienced a burgeoning of art, culture, science and exploration. In the words of the historian Simon Schama, 'There is perhaps no other example of a complete and highly original civilisation springing up in so short a time in so small a territory.' Though its lustre may have been dulled by the passage of four centuries, the glint of the Golden Age shines through the contributions of subsequent generations.

Population explosion

In the first half of the 17th century, the city's population soared from 60,000 to nearly 220,000. In addition to accepting Catholics from countries that persecuted these traditional Christians, Protestant Amsterdam welcomed Huguenot and Walloon immigrants from France, Lutherans from Germany and Jews from Germany and Portugal, thereby setting a precedent for tolerance. Moreover, numerous inhabitants of colonised territories, in Africa, the Far and Middle East, and the West Indies, migrated to the city, which established a reputation as Europe's most cosmopolitan city. The resultant ethnic mix can still be seen.

Equally significant was the establishment, in 1602, of the Verenigde Oostindische Compagnie (VOC), the United East India Company, which handled trade with the Orient; its counterpart for the West Indies was founded in 1621. The Bank of Amsterdam opened its doors in 1609 and the Amsterdam Stock Exchange in 1611. The long and difficult sea journeys to the country's far-flung possessions required stout ships, and the VOC's shipyard at Oostenburg in Amsterdam became the world's largest industrial complex.

The wonderful art that emerged at this time was the direct result of the wealth of the Dutch middle class. In

Café In 't Aepjen.

contrast with the artists of the Italian Renaissance, who were dependent on commissions from powerful patrons, Dutch painters could sell their works to the highest bidder, who was very often an ordinary, if rich, citizen.

Loss of empire
By the 18th century a decline, both aesthetic and commercial, was evident. Though international trade was the focal point of Dutch wealth, the country was not destined to be a long-standing colonial force in the way that Britain and France were.

In 1795 Amsterdam was invaded by the French and in 1808 Napoleon installed his brother, Louis, as king of the Netherlands, with Amsterdam as his capital. Following Napoleon's ignominious exit from a Europe that he had dominated for 20 years, the Netherlands' northern and southern provinces were united, though the latter achieved independence as Belgium in 1831. Holland did manage to retain much of its empire, the fruits of which (mainly coffee, rubber and timber) remained vital staples of the economy until well into the 20th century.

World War I and World War II
The country sided with neither the Allied nor Axis powers in World War I, but this neutrality made little impression on the Nazis, who invaded on 10 May, 1940. The most famous Dutch victim of the subsequent Holocaust was Anne Frank, whose Diary is a moving testaments to the life of a Jewish family in hiding. Today Anne Frank Huis is one of the city's busiest tourist sites.

Post-war period
The country was still recovering from the long years of Nazi occupation when disaster struck. In 1953 a combination of bad weather conditions sent the North Sea crashing through the sea defences in Zeeland. More than 1,800 people lost their lives. Canals, windmills, dikes and polders all tell the story of reclamation from the sea.

In the post-war period, Amsterdam developed a reputation for social liberalism with sex, drugs and squatting to the fore.

The Netherlands joined the European Union (then the European Economic Community) in 1957. Their natural strengths in agricultural production and trade have ensured their success in the alliance. Amsterdam has become one of the premier tourist cities in the world, trading on its historic centre and its wealth of artistic collections. Today it operates much as it did in the Golden Age, with banking, trade and modern 'pilgrims' (in the form of tourists) ensuring it remains a wealthy city.

Twenty-first century challenges
The murder of film-maker Theo van Gogh in 2004 for his anti-Muslim views sparked race-relations clashes and the inclusion of controversial right-wing pol-

A wedding party on the canal.

itician Geert Wilders in the coalition government in 2010 did nothing to ease social tensions. The Dutch economy – the fifth largest in the Eurozone – did not escape the euro crisis. To the casual tourist, however, multiracial Amsterdam seems remarkably well integrated and there is little sign of the financial downturn. The city has seen the opening of swish new hotels, Michelin-starred restaurants and luxury designer stores, and the restoration of arts venues, including the stunning transformation of the Rijksmuseum. Along the waterfront ambitious new buildings have sprouted in what were formerly derelict docklands.

DON'T LEAVE AMSTERDAM WITHOUT...

Leaving Amsterdam. Although the city is a delight, try to find time to take the train to The Hague (see page 86), or perhaps feel utterly Dutch and take a bicycle out across the IJsselmeer (see page 83).

Seeing *Sunflowers*. Van Gogh's famous painting *Sunflowers* is among the 200 paintings – and another 500-plus drawings – held by the Van Gogh Museum, the world's most comprehensive collection of work by this tortured genius. See page 41.

Visiting Anne Frank Huis. There may be long queues for the city's most visited attraction, and it may be crowded and over surprisingly quickly, but the time spent seeing the small secret annex where Anne Frank and her family hid from the Nazis will stay with you forever. See page 27.

Venturing into the red-light district. There aren't many cities in the world where the red-light district is one of the major attractions. Amsterdam's is right in the city centre, so take advantage and satisfy your curiosity in a fairly safe way – though always watch out for pickpockets. See page 75.

Meeting Rembrandt. Although his great works, including *The Night Watch*, are on display in the Rijksmuseum (see page 37), a greater appreciation of Rembrandt the man can be had if you also visit the house where he lived and worked (see page 65).

Getting on the water. The city's canals are a pleasure to look at but you get a different take on Amsterdam when you see it from the water, and get a glimpse of canal life. You can do this on one of the popular canal boat tours (see page 80), or perhaps be a little more adventurous and rent a canal bike for yourself (see page 52).

Tucking into a *rijsttafel*. The 'rice table' is the Indonesian equivalent of a meze and allows you the chance to feast on many different dishes and sample the variety of Indonesian cuisine which is so popular throughout the Netherlands. See page 19.

Buying a diamond. Well, perhaps think about buying a diamond or doing your research at one of the diamond factories like Gassan Diamonds (see page 21) where you can learn what to look for in the future when you are buying diamonds.

Albert Cuyp Market.

CLIMATE

The Netherlands has unpredictable weather patterns similar to those of Britain, characterised by cold, wet winters and warm, wet summers. You can, however, have wonderful sunny days at any time of year, and Amsterdammers always hope for long periods of bright, cold winter spells.

POPULATION

Amsterdam's population is almost equally split between people of Dutch origin and people with immigrant backgrounds, though in many cases these go back several generations. Most come from former Dutch colonies like Surinam and Indonesia, and there are a number of immigrant workers, too, from countries such as Turkey and Morocco. Its tolerant attitudes also draw a lot of young people, either permanently or temporarily.

LOCAL CUSTOMS

Tipping on restaurant and bar bills is not usually necessary, as by law the bill amount must include the service charge and taxes. If you want to leave some change on the table that's fine, but no need to pay an extra 10–20 percent. English is very widely spoken, so you're not likely to need a phrase book, although using a few local courtesy words is always appreciated. It's customary for friends to greet each other with three kisses, Italian-style, starting on the right cheek. One thing to watch for is that dinner is usually eaten early in Amsterdam, typically starting at 6–7pm. You'll still find places open later at night, but many kitchens close by about 10pm.

POLITICS AND ECONOMICS

The country's full title, The Kingdom of the Netherlands, shows that it is a monarchy, but this being the Netherlands, it's a fairly liberal monarchy where the monarch is usually regarded with great affection. Currently that is King Willem-Alexander. In contrast, the Netherlands democracy embraces all kinds of political parties. For example, a new party representing pensioners and called 50PLUS won two seats in the 2012 election and four in the 2017 election. In 2017, the 150 Parliamentary seats were split between 13 different parties. A new coalition government headed by Mark Rutte of the conservative/liberal VVD (People's Party for Freedom and Democracy) was finally formed in October 2017 following 225 days of talks.

Amsterdam is also the financial and business capital of the Netherlands, and despite the world's economic woes it has a comparatively healthy economy, helped by having Europe's fourth-largest port, one of Europe's largest Stock Exchanges and receiving about 20 million visitors a year.

Cycling through De Pijp.

Café Sappho.

TOP TIPS FOR EXPLORING AMSTERDAM

Start the day early. If you want to see top attractions, including the Anne Frank Huis and the Van Gogh Museum, it's better to get up early and arrive maybe 20–30 minutes before the doors open. It may seem like a long wait, but it won't be as long as you would have if you arrived an hour later.

Pack for all seasons. No matter what the weather forecast says, for Amsterdam it's best to pack assuming you may well experience all four seasons over the course of a few days. Take both sunscreen and an umbrella in summer, and plan to dress in layers at any time of year. Nights can be cold, so be ready with a sweater even in summer.

Choose your dates. There are lots of fun festivals and events in Amsterdam throughout the year (see page 112), so check what's happening when you're thinking of visiting. If you can adjust your dates to coincide with an event, whether it's Gay Pride or the King's Birthday, do it. Amsterdammers know how to have a good time.

Allow time for shopping. Allow yourself time not just for regular street shopping, but when visiting museums too. The Rijksmuseum shop is huge and carries unusual items that the museum has commissioned from local designers, while the Van Gogh Museum shop is equally impressive with creative and tasteful items in among the predictable fridge magnets and postcards.

Master public transport. Although it's easy to see Amsterdam on foot, and you can walk across the city centre in 30 minutes, when the skies open and it starts raining you'll be glad you picked up that public transport map at the tourist office and bought your public transport chip card in advance, so you can hop on the right tram going in the right direction.

Try a variety of dining. Don't stick to what you know you like to eat. There's an incredible range of eating experiences to be had in Amsterdam, so try them. Save a bit of money one day by eating street food like *haring* (herring) or *friet* (French fries) smothered in mayonnaise. Then splurge the next day with dinner at one of the city's Michelin-starred restaurants. In-between there's good, inexpensive food to be had in some of the brown cafés, where you'll also get a great atmosphere. And try at least one Indonesian meal too.

Research your accommodation. Amsterdam has a wide choice of places to stay, from budget hostels to five-star opulence (see page 92). It also has some absolutely wonderful historic canalside buildings that have been converted into accommodation, sometimes boutique and sometimes basic. But before booking into one of those historic buildings, check where your room is and if there's a lift. Some people may find it difficult when they discover they are on the fourth floor and there's no lift!

Raw herring is a delicacy in Holland.

FOOD AND DRINK

Although traditional Dutch food has a reputation for being dull, Amsterdam's immigrant population ensures a rainbow of dining experiences. From street food to gourmet, via some affordable but innovative restaurants, you can eat very well here.

Traditional Dutch cuisine includes a limited range of dishes, yet eating out in Amsterdam can be one of the highlights of the trip. The reason? Many of the city's more than 100 nationalities have brought their own unique culinary delights to Amsterdam's restaurants. You could stay in the city for over a month and not eat the same style of food twice.

LOCAL CUISINE

Traditional Dutch food is seasonal and based on whatever was harvested from the land or the sea, with light summer dishes and hearty, filling winter foods. Arable farms abound in the countryside, and meat dishes do not generally play a major part in Dutch cuisine. Fish and dairy produce are considerably more prevalent.

The Dutch breakfast (*ontbijt*) is a hearty one. Slices of ham and cheese, and perhaps boiled eggs with various breads and jam or honey are accompanied by strong milky coffee.

Although Amsterdammers are moving towards lighter, healthier fare, they still enjoy lunch-time *pannenkoeken*,

pancakes thicker than the French crêpe and made fresh as you order them. You can have savoury ones (with eggs and bacon, for instance) or sweet toppings, with fruit, chocolate and cream, or perhaps even one of each. *Uitsmijter* is another interesting and popular lunch dish, served in Dutch homes and in cafés. It consists of a slice of bread toasted on one side, onto which a slice of ham and a fried egg are added.

Broodjes or sandwiches are available with a vast range of fillings. The local ham and Dutch cheeses are probably the most authentic if you want to eat local, and the combination is delicious eaten hot in a *toastje* or toasted sandwich.

Winter dishes are warming and hearty. Start with a bowl of *erwtensoep*, a thick pea soup with chunks of sausage. Served with heavy bread or pumpernickel, it constitutes a meal in itself. The other main type of soup is *bruine bonen soep* made with red kidney beans. This may then be followed by *stamppot*, a purée of potatoes and vegetables (usually kale or cabbage) served with slices of *rookworst* (thick

Wheels of Zaanlander cheese.

smoked sausage), or *hutspot*, made with beef.

Fish

Fish (*vis*) has been a mainstay of the Dutch diet for many generations. Try halibut (*heilbot*), cod (*kabeljauw*) or haddock (*schelvis*), all of which come from the North Sea off the Dutch coast. Local oysters (*oesters*) and mussels (*mosselen*) are especially good, and smoked eel (*gerookte paling*) is a Dutch delicacy. A dish that harks back to the Calvinists, and which is light on the palate, is a basic meal of plaice (*schol*) with vegetables, where the fish is grilled and served with butter. You'll also find freshwater fish, called 'sweetwater fish' (*zoetwatervis*) by the Dutch, from some canals and rivers.

Cheese

Cheese (*kaas*) is eaten more often at breakfast or lunch rather than with dinner. Both Gouda and Edam, named after the towns where they are produced, are easily identifiable, being round in shape and covered in red (for export) or yellow wax that keeps the cheese airtight, allowing it to be kept for many months.

Desserts

The Dutch aren't known for their sweet tooth, although most cafés and restaurants will have *appelgebak* (apple pie) on the menu. You will also find *stroopwafels*, thin round waffles filled with golden syrup and butter; and *poffertjes*, small, shell-shaped pieces of dough, fried in butter and sugar.

WHERE TO EAT

Street food

Street food has always been popular in Amsterdam. *Friet* (French fries) are eaten at any time of day. They are thickly cut and served with a spoonful of thick mayonnaise. You'll see the vendors' stalls in squares or on street corners.

The typical Dutch way to eat herring is to take the tail in one hand, hold it above your mouth and slowly eat it in bites, so that the herring gradually disappears and only the tail is left. Amsterdammers often prefer herring chopped and served with raw chopped onions.

Eetcafés

An *eetcafé* is somewhere between a café and a restaurant, perhaps more equivalent to a French bistro. It will usually serve simple meals, though some *eetcafés* offer quite sophisticated dishes, but the name distinguishes it from a café, where only drinks are served.

Ethnic restaurants

Amsterdam offers food from almost every corner of the globe, so don't be afraid to try places that may not look too promising at first glance. Indone-

Erwtensoep (pea and sausage soup).

sian cuisine in particular is hot here – in more ways than one – and should be on everyone's dining list.

Fine dining

In 2018 there were 18 restaurants in Amsterdam with one or two Michelin stars. If you want the fine dining experience then you can have it, with some focusing on Dutch ingredients and others a more traditional French cuisine style.

Attractions

If planning where to eat, don't forget the attractions that you'll also be seeing. The Rijksmuseum, for example, has an excellent restaurant which focuses on Dutch ingredients and invites guest chefs in to oversee the menu. And, like many of the city's museums, it also has a café if you want a simpler meal. The Artis Zoo has several cafés and restaurants, and scattered around the grounds you'll find the traditional Dutch *bakfietsen*: a combination of bike and street food stall. The organic café at the Hortus Botanicus is situated in The Orangery, one of the loveliest café settings in the city. At NEMO you can take your own picnic to enjoy on the roof terrace, which has spectacular views.

DRINKS

The Dutch love their bars. You'll find one on almost every street corner; they are warm, welcoming places where you can sit for hours. The staple place to socialise is the *bruine kroeg* (brown café), so called because of their brown-stained walls, low lighting and smoky interiors. They sell alcohol, coffee and light snacks, and are as much an institution as the pub is in Britain. These cafés define the Dutch word *gezelligheid*, which means a state of cosiness or conviviality. This is where local people come for a few beers after work, to play cards, engage in political debates and tell tall tales.

Traditional Dutch bars have historically centred on two products. Beer is one and *jenever* (pronounced 'yen-ey-fer') the other. At one time, distillers and brewers had tasting houses (*proeflokalen*) for their products where buyers would convene to test the latest brews or compare vintages. Today, there are only a few of these remaining in the city and they always serve a range of other drinks, in addition to their traditional one.

As well as beer and *jenever*, most bars also serve wine, coffee and soft drinks. Coffee is the lifeblood of Amsterdam. The strong black short serving of fresh brew – and it must be fresh – is sold in cafés and bars all across the city.

Beer

Dutch-produced beer is generally a pils variety, slightly stronger than Brit-

Indonesian Rijsttafel.

Knocking back a jenever.

ish lager or American beer. If you order beer by the glass it will usually come in a 33cl (12fl oz) measure, served chilled. The two fingers of froth that crown your beer are traditional; they are levelled with the top of the glass with a white plastic spatula. Heineken is the Netherlands' best-known beer and the former brewery has been converted into the Heineken Experience, with light-hearted self-guided tours, complemented by a couple of free beers at the end.

Jenever

Jenever (or *genever*) is the Dutch spirit from which gin, and its name, is derived. Like gin it has a predominantly juniper taste, and is thought to date back to at least the 16th century. If you don't like a strong juniper taste, ask for a *jonge jenever*, or young *jenever*, which has a slightly more neutral taste to it. *Oude* or old *jenever* has often been aged in barrels like whisky or bourbon, leading to more complex flavours.

Whatever you do, don't ask for a *jenever* and tonic. *Jenever* is usually drunk neat and served in a tulip-shaped glass that's completely full. You may need to take your first sip while the glass is on the table or counter, before lifting it to your lips. Bars often keep their *jenever* bottles in the freezer, to provide an ice-cold shot, though you can also ask for it on the rocks.

Indonesian Cuisine

The expansion of Dutch interests in the Golden Age brought a wealth of new ingredients and flavourings from the Far East. This added interest to native dishes, such as the Dutch habit of sprinkling nutmeg on cooked vegetables, but also, over the centuries, close ties with what is now Indonesia created a second Dutch national dish – *rijsttafel* (literally translated as 'rice table'). There are numerous Indonesian restaurants throughout the city offering *rijsttafel* with 10, 15 or 20 dishes. If you don't want a full *rijsttafel*, order *nasi rames*, a smaller selection of dishes served with rice – an ideal choice for lunch.

Rijsttafel is a Dutch interpretation of Indonesian cuisine, which became accepted both in the old colonies and in the Netherlands as a meal in itself. Take a serving of rice and put it in the middle of your plate, then take small amounts of the spicy meat, fish and vegetable dishes, and place them around the outside of the rice. The small courses balance one another in taste, texture and heat (spiciness) to excite the palate.

The standard dishes include *babi* (pork), *daging bronkos* (roast meat in coconut milk), goreng kering (pimento and fish paste) and small skewers of meat (*satay*) with peanut sauce. Any dish that is labelled sambal is guaranteed to be hot (spicy), but hot dishes are tempered with cooling ones such as marinated fruits and vegetables.

Diamonds are forever.

SHOPPING

Amsterdam is a great city for shopping but not in the same way as New York, London or Paris. Although it has plenty of upscale designer and department stores, the city's intimate, eccentric lifestyle is reflected in its more interesting shops.

The city's best shopping options are to be found in offbeat speciality shops, highly individualistic outlets and in a diverse array of flourishing street markets. If you keep your eyes open as you walk around the city, you will doubtless appreciate that the consumer options in Holland, and Amsterdam in particular, are boundless.

Thursday evening is *koopavond* (late-shopping), when most shops are open till 9pm. Otherwise, opening hours can vary enormously, though 8am/9am to 5pm/6pm, Monday to Saturday is typical. It's also fairly common for stores to open on a Sunday afternoon. Against that, they often don't open till later in the morning on the nights when they stay open late, and don't always open at their regular time on Monday mornings either.

SHOPPING AREAS

Kalverstraat
Kalverstraat is Amsterdam's most popular shopping street. It is full of cheap and cheerful outlets, supplemented by a sprinkling of higher-priced designer stores. While the actual street begins at the Dam and runs to Muntplein, the shopping zone includes its continuation across the Dam in Nieuwendijk, and the adjacent Rokin. The Dam features several department stores, including the Bijenkorf (Amsterdam's best), Peek & Cloppenburg and Maison de Bonneterie.

Beyond the mass of clothes, sports and shoe shops, this district features a branch of the Waterstone's bookshop chain, at Kalverstraat 152. On Rokin, one of the most interesting shops is the PGC Hajenius tobacconist at No. 96. If you like your Havanas from a humidor, or want a traditional clay pipe for a souvenir, this is the place for you.

Pieter Cornelisz Hooftstraat
The best place for designer clothes is Pieter Cornelisz Hoofstraat – better known as the 'PC Hooft' – and the adjoining Van Baerlestraat. You will find this district in the Museum Quarter, not far from the rear of the Rijksmuseum. Some of the highly-rated outlets on the PC Hooft and Van Baerlestraat include: Azzurro, Chanel, Dior, Louis Vuitton, Prada and Pauw (and Pauw Junior for the well-dressed offspring). Here you

Bulbs for sale at the Bloemenmarkt.

will also find a branch of the Belgian chocolatier Godiva.

Leidsestraat

Leidsestraat runs from Leidseplein, through Koningsplein, and on to Heiligeweg before it joins up with the southern end of Kalverstraat. It is actually an upmarket extension of Kalverstraat, with outlets such as Ecco and Abercrombie & Fitch. If you're looking for footwear, one of the city's most interesting options is Shoebaloo at Koningsplein 7. The Spiegelgracht Canal near Leidseplein leads onto Nieuwe Spiegelstraat, which has become an enclave of quality antiques shops.

Markets

Amsterdam loves street markets. Some are permanent, others appear on a day or two each week. The best markets are: Albert Cuyp Market, Albert Cuypstraat (Mon–Sat); Bio Market, Noordermarkt (Sat), which specialises in organically grown fruit and vegetables; Bloemenmarkt, Singel (daily), the famous floating flower market, where prices are competitive and the flowers excellent; Garden Market, Amstelveld (Mon); Textile Market, Noordermarkt (Mon morning); Thorbecke Art Market, Thorbeckeplein (Mar–Oct Sun only); Waterlooplein Rommelmarkt (Mon–Sat), the city's premier flea market, where everything and anything goes (on Sunday in summer the merchandise is very big on antiques and second-hand books).

DUTCH PRODUCTS

Dutch products that make good buys and souvenirs include the following: flower bulbs (but be warned that, to import these to some countries, you will be required to show a phytosanitary certificate); Delft and Makkum pottery (for high-quality originals, Delft products are labelled 'De Porcelyne Fles', their Makkum equivalents, 'Tichelaars'); Koninklijke Leerdam crystal; pewter; cheese from specialist shops; chocolates from Droste, Van Houten and Verkade; antiques; and diamonds.

DIAMONDS

Amsterdam prides itself on being the 'City of Diamonds'. There is a certain amount of marketing hype about this, as Antwerp's diamond trade is worth six times as much. Still, a billion dollars or so of annual sales add up to a sparkling business, and Amsterdam makes it fun to shell out for precious stones. You are unlikely to find much in the way of bargains, though.

Shops associated with the Amsterdam Diamond Foundation are reputable, and they offer tours in which you can see diamond cutting and polishing. The relevant shops are: Amsterdam Diamond Centre, Rokin 1; Coster, Paulus Potterstraat 2; Gassan, Nieuwe Uilenburgerstraat 173; Van Moppes, Potterstraat 2–8.

Map of Amsterdam by Johannes Blaeu, c.1652.

HISTORY: KEY DATES

From its beginnings as a marshland fishing village through to being capital of the Dutch Empire, through the joys of its Golden Age and the dark days of the war, Amsterdam has always been a city with a story.

THE FOUNDING OF THE CITY

c.1200	Herring fishermen settle at the mouth of the River Amstel.
c.1220	The first dam is built to hold back the tidal waters of the Zuiderzee at a settlement that becomes known as Aemstelledamme.
1300	The Bishop of Utrecht grants Amsterdam its city charter.
1334	Work begins on the Oude Kerk, the city's first parish church.
1345	'Miracle of the Host' – a dying man regurgitates the Communion bread and it remains intact when thrown on a fire.
1395	The city's first town hall is built in Dam Square.
1400	Work begins on the Nieuwe Kerk.
1414	Amsterdam becomes Holland's biggest town, with a population of 12,000.
1452	Fire destroys most of the timber-built city.
1480	Defensive walls are built.
1535	Protestant Anabaptists occupy the town hall. The revolt is suppressed and Catholicism imposed.
1566	The city's first Calvinist church is established.
1578	The city surrenders and the churches and government are taken over by Calvinists.

THE GOLDEN AGE

1602	Establishment of the United East India Company, with its headquarters in Amsterdam.
1611	Amsterdam Stock Exchange opens.
1632	Establishment of the Athenaeum Illustre, which later becomes Amsterdam University.
1642	Rembrandt paints his most famous work *The Night Watch*.
1648	Work begins on the new town hall.

The inauguration of King Willem–Alexander.

1650   The city's population reaches 220,000.

INVASIONS

1745   Schools for needy children are established.

1806   Napoleon abolishes the republic and proclaims his brother Louis as king of the Netherlands, with Amsterdam as his capital.

1845   Pro-democracy riots lead to the establishment of a constitution.

1876   North Sea Canal opens.

1928   Amsterdam hosts the Olympic Games.

1940   Nazi Germany invades and occupies Holland.

1941   Workers, led by dockers, strike for two days in protest against the deportation of the city's Jews.

1942   Anne Frank and her family go into hiding.

1945   Amsterdam is liberated by the Allies.

TODAY'S AMSTERDAM

1965   Anti-establishment Provos win seats on the city council.

1992   Amsterdammers vote to curb car use in the city.

2002   The euro becomes the country's official currency.

2004   After making a film critical of Islam, director Theo van Gogh is murdered in Amsterdam.

2007   City Council introduces the controversial Project 1012 to cut the number of cannabis cafés and brothel windows in the red-light district.

2010   Amsterdam's ring of canals receives Unesco World Heritage Site status.

2013   Abdication of Queen Beatrix of the Netherlands and inauguration of King Willem-Alexander. 400th anniversary of the Canal Ring. Minimum legal age for a prostitute in Amsterdam is raised from 18 to 21.

2014   Malaysian Airlines plane heading from Amsterdam to Kuala Lumpur is shot down over Ukraine, killing 193 Dutch citizens.

2017   Prime Minister Mark Rutte forms a new coalition government after 225 days of talks.

2018   Following years of work, Amsterdam's Noord-Zuidlijn metro line is inaugurated.

BEST ROUTES

1. The Golden Age Canals 26
2. The Principal Squares 32
3. The Museum Quarter 37
4. The Old Centre (The Wallen) 43
5. The Zoo District 46
6. The Harbour 49
7. The Canals by Pedal Bike 52
8. Amsterdam by Tram 54
9. By Bicycle along the River Amstel 57
10. The Jordaan 60
11. The Jewish Quarter 63
12. Amsterdamse Bos 66
13. Leidseplein 69
14. Rembrandtplein 72
15. Red-Light District 75
16. Haarlem and Zandvoort 78
17. The IJsselmeer by Bike 83
18. The Hague 86

THE GOLDEN AGE CANALS

*This route follows the concentric semi-circle of 16th- and 17th-century canals –
Singel, Herengracht, Keizersgracht and Prinsengracht. Highlights include the
Anne Frank Huis, several museums and some offbeat stores. A substantial amount
of walking is involved but there are lots of 'time out' options en route.*

DISTANCE: 4.5km (2.8 miles)
TIME: a full day
START: Haarlemmer Houttuinen/Korte
Prinsengracht junction
END: Willet-Holthuysen Museum
POINTS TO NOTE: If there's a long
queue to visit the Anne Frank Huis
when you arrive, return another day and
try to be there for opening time.

Amsterdam's canals – and especially
the grander canals built in the Golden
Age of the 16th and 17th centuries –
are what the city is all about for many
visitors. They are indeed splendid
sights, lined with tall, elegant and historic buildings. If you walk in Amsterdam you can't avoid walking by canals,
but some are more historic than others
and this walk ties several of the best
together, while also including several of
the city's main sights.

Begin west of Centraal Station at the
junction of Haarlemmer Houttuinen and
Korte Prinsengracht. If you are arriving
from Centraal Station, walk to the starting point, along Prins Hendrikkade to
Haarlemmer Houttuinen.

CANALS

Three of the canals around which this
itinerary is based are lasting testimony
to the city's 17th-century Golden Age.
It is unfortunate that the glories of that
heyday have been tarnished by the less
positive aspects of contemporary life
– namely noise, pollution and parking
problems – but these minor annoy-
ances do not completely break the connection with those Calvinist burghers
who made the Golden Age shine.

Starting on the east side of the Korte
Prinsengracht, at the junction with
Haarlemmer Houttuinen, walk along
the narrow canal to the corner of **Brouwersgracht** (Brewers' Canal) and **Prinsengracht**. Note how all of the former
brewery warehouses along Brouwers-
grachthave been converted into
expensive apartments. At the junction
of the two canals are a couple of recommended spots, should you fancy a
breakfast snack: **Café Tabac** and **'t**

Amsterdam by night.

Papeneiland, see ❶ and ❷. Both are brown cafés (*bruine kroegen*) – old, traditional-style Dutch bars known for their colour, which comes from the wood being stained by centuries of smoke.

MARKET SQUARE

Cross Brouwersgracht by the bridge here, then switch to the west (right) bank of Prinsengracht. The first stop is **Noordermarkt** and the **Noorderkerk** (North Church) ❶ that stands in the market square. On Saturday Noordermarkt hosts a **Bird Market** and a **Farmers' Market** selling organically-grown produce. On Monday morning there's a textiles and second-hand market here. Some gables overlooking the square feature agricultural images – of cows, chickens and the like – that recall the square's historical role as a market. The Noorderkerk, designed by Hendrick de Keyser, the Golden Age's master church builder, dates to 1623.

Continue along Prinsengracht to the bridge at Prinsenstraat, and turn left along this short street, which is lined with cafés and restaurants. Cross over the **Keizersgracht** bridge – note the houseboats moored on either side – onto Heerenstraat and continue to **Herengracht** before turning right along the canal.

ANNE FRANK HUIS

Turn right on Leliegracht, go up onto Prinsengracht and turn left to visit the **Anne Frank Huis** ❷ (Anne Frank House; Prinsengracht 263; www.annefrank.org; daily Apr–Oct 9am–10pm, Nov–Mar 9am–7pm, Sat until 9pm), one of Amsterdam's most popular 'attractions'. This is the house in which the teenage Jewish diarist, Anne Frank (1929–45) hid with her family (and two other families) for more than two years during World War II before being captured by the Nazis, at whose hands she died of hunger and disease in Bergen-Belsen concentration camp.

Generally, the earlier you arrive the better, because the queues are sometimes very long. In summer especially you might have to wait in line for an hour or more, unless you go after 6pm.

Most people consider the wait worthwhile. Not that there is much to see inside: that's the whole point. The

---

Lean Times

As you stroll along the canalsides you will notice that there are very few houses standing absolutely upright – in fact, some seem to lean at a precarious angle. Don't assume that this is because of subsidence; most were designed to tilt towards the canal so that goods could be winched to the upper floors without crashing into the side of the house. Unfortunately, some of them tilted too much, resulting in the 1565 building code, which limited the inclination to 1 in 25.

Anne Frank Huis.

rooms in which the Franks hid are as bare as they were on the day the family was betrayed and taken to the death camp. But it is not difficult, using your imagination and powers of empathy, to put yourself in Anne's situation, awakening as a young woman, and telling her secret thoughts to the diary. Her life was extinguished; her spirit lives on.

The Anne Frank Huis also acts as an education centre and resource for political and philosophical groups fighting oppression in the present day.

One of three **Stromma** pedal boats moorings is on Prinsengracht outside the Anne Frank Huis, so if you fancy a more light-hearted activity at this point, spend an hour pottering about on the water (see also route 7).

WESTERKERK

Continue a few steps to **Westermarkt** and the **Westerkerk** (church; www.westerkerk.nl; Mon–Fri 10am–3pm, Sun open for services only, Apr–Oct also Sat 10am–3pm; free; tower: guided tours Apr–Oct Mon–Sat 10am–8pm), a Renaissance-style church built between 1620 and 1631. The latter date marked the opening of its tower, the **Westertoren**, which is surmounted by the blue, red and gold crown of the Holy Roman Empire, a symbol bestowed by the Austrian Emperor Maximilian. Although Rembrandt was interred in the church, no trace of his tomb has ever been found. Also on Westermarkt is a sculpture of Anne Frank and the marble triangles of the **Homomonument**, dedicated to the gay and lesbian victims of persecution down the centuries.

Across the street at Westermarkt 33, on the corner of Prinsengracht, is a lunch option, the **Kalkhoven**, see ③. Before continuing along Prinsengracht, you might want to make a short diversion, to the right, to Rozengracht 17, to visit the **Blue Gold Fish**, an intriguingly offbeat jewellery-cum-gift shop with a style all its own.

NINE LITTLE STREETS

Continue along Prinsengracht, past the Pulitzer Hotel, to Reestraat. From here, go down to Keizersgracht, turn right and continue as far as Wolvenstraat. These connecting streets are some of the so-called **Negen Straatjes** (Nine Little Streets), which are noted for their many interesting and sometimes offbeat shops.

At Herengracht go right to Wijde Heisteeg, then left once again to the Singel and on to Spui. This square is quite fascinating (see route 2). You might however want to adjourn for a coffee break here at **Café Hoppe**, see ④ (Spuistraat 18–20), another traditional brown café.

Either way, walk alongside the far bank of Singel to the **Bloemenmarkt** ⑤ (Flower Market), which is one of Amsterdam's most special sites. It's like a botanical garden set along the canal,

The Homomonument.   The secret annex.

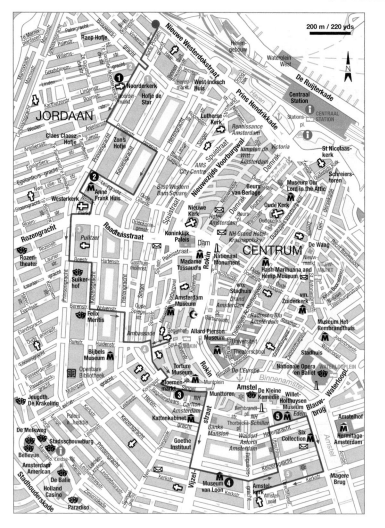

Bloemenmarkt.

with heaps of flowers changing hands. This is probably the best – and is certainly the most atmospheric – place at which to buy cut flowers and bulbs. You are now at **Muntplein**, a busy tram intersection, and its **Munttoren** (Mint Tower). The base of the tower used to be part of the Reguliers Gate in the city wall, and in 1620 Hendrick de Keyser added the ornate, lead-covered bell tower whose bells sing out gaily every Tuesday and Friday at 12.30pm and 1pm respectively.

Turn right along Vijzelstraat to Herengracht to visit the **Kattenkabinet** (Cat Museum; Herengracht 497; www.kattenkabinet.nl; Mon–Fri 10am–5pm, Sat–Sun noon–5pm). This museum is dedicated to depictions of our feline friends. Sculptures, paintings and prints

Café Hoppe.

show the role of the cat in art and culture through the centuries. The Golden-Age merchants' houses ranged along the bend in the canal at this point give rise to this neighbourhood's name: the Golden Bend.

PATRICIAN RESIDENCES

Proceed up Vijzelstraat to Keizersgracht and turn left to visit the **Museum van Loon** ❹ (Keizersgracht 672; www.museumvanloon.nl; daily 10am–5pm). This museum gives you a glimpse behind the gables at what a patrician house – in this case a double house dating from 1672 – of the era immediately following the Golden Age would have looked like. Its restored period rooms are filled with richly decorated panelling, stucco work, mirrors, fireplaces, furnishings, porcelain, medallions, chandeliers, rugs, and so forth. The marble staircase, complete with intricately designed balustrade, is itself a masterpiece.

Continue across Reguliersgracht to Utrechtsestraat, a fascinating shopping street with some good restaurants, such as the Indonesian **Tempo Doeloe**, see ❺. To see another richly-decorated, 17th-century patrician canal house, head north to the junction with Herengracht and turn right to the **Willet-Holthuysen Museum** ❺ (Herengracht 605; www.willetholthuysen.nl; Mon–Fri 10am–5pm, Sat–Sun 11am–5pm). Check out the dining salon, with a table

Museum Van Loon.

Magere Brug on the Amstel.

set under the chandelier for what looks like a pretty fancy meal. A walk to the end of Herengracht is rewarded by a picturesque scene at the **River Amstel**.

Afterwards, if you want to treat yourself, return to Utrechtsestraat and dine at Tempo Doeloe ⑤, or one of the numerous other excellent restaurants (Dutch, ethnic, seafood and vegetarian) situated on this long street.

Food and Drink

① CAFÉ TABAC

Brouwersgracht 101; tel: 020-622 4413; Sat 11am–3am, Sun 11am–1am, Mon–Thu noon–1am, Fri noon–3am; €

This straightforward brown café serves an inexpensive international menu with such dishes as Taiwanese salad, chicken curry, *gado-gado*, a *rijstaffel*, and a range of vegetarian dishes too. Drinks range from coffee to cocktails via seasonal beers and a selection of *jenevers*.

② 'T PAPENEILAND

Prinsengracht 2; tel: 020-624 1989; www. papeneiland.nl; Mon–Thu 10am–1am, Fri–Sat until 3am; €€

This historic café is an Amsterdam institution, dating from 1642. Among the people who have enjoyed its cosy interior, covered with Delft blue tiles, is Bill Clinton. They're noted for their home-made apple pie, and apparently Bill Clinton loved it.

③ KALKHOVEN

Prinsengracht 283; tel: 020-624 8649; www.cafekalkhoven.nl; lunch served daily 11am–4pm, café open Mon–Thu 9am–1am, Fri–Sat 9am–2am, Sun 10am–10pm; €

This traditional old brown café first opened its doors in 1670 and looks like it hasn't changed much since. It's a characterful place with rugs on the tables and hard drinkers around the bar. There's an extensive beer list and meatballs is one of their lunch specialities.

④ CAFÉ HOPPE

Spui 18–20; tel: 020-420 4420; http://cafehoppe.com; Sun–Thu 8am–1am, Fri–Sat until 2am; €

One of Amsterdam's classic brown cafés, even visited by the former Queen, Beatrix. It's been in the same location since 1670. It serves breakfast and lunch, and has a wide beer menu and a fine list of *jenevers* and liqueurs.

⑤ TEMPO DOELOE

Utrechtsestraat 75; tel: 0618 439 251; www.tempodoeloerestaurant.nl; Mon–Tue 6pm–midnight, Wed noon–midnight, Thu–Sat noon–1am; €€

One of the best and busiest Indonesian restaurants in town, with a choice of *rijstaffels* that can go up to 25 different dishes, including a vegetarian option. Friendly staff will advise on the heat level of spices.

Nationaal Monument.

THE PRINCIPAL SQUARES

Highlights of this tour include tranquil Spui and the adjacent Begijnhof, glitzy Rembrandtplein, the Kalverstraat shopping area and the Spiegelkwartier antiques district. Finish the day at the lively Leidseplein.

DISTANCE: 2.5km (1.6 miles)
TIME: A leisurely day
START: The Dam
END: Leidseplein
POINTS TO NOTE: This is a flexible tour and could be done without stops in 30 minutes, but there's a great deal to see on the way.

To really get to know Amsterdam you need to get to know its squares. They not only give you an insight into city life, they act as good navigation points. Once you know the main squares, like the grand Dam and the rowdy Leidseplein, you'll be able to find your way around the city a lot better, and will find its public transport system makes more sense. In addition, this walk takes you to the beguiling Begijnhof, a courtyard that is one of the city's true hidden gems.

Start at the Dam, which can be reached by taking any of the following trams: 2, 4, 11, 12, 13, 14, 17 and 24 from Centraal Station.

THE DAM

The **Dam**, which isn't a dam any more, marks the spot where the first dam was built on the River Amstel c.1220, an event that led to the establishment of the city. Now it is Amsterdam's most monumental square. Before you set out from the Dam, you might want to have breakfast at the **Grand Hotel Krasnapolsky**, see ➊. If so, it's well worth taking a turn around the ground floor of the hotel, which was opened in 1866 by a former Polish tailor; the restored Wintertuin (Winter Garden) restaurant is an extravagant example of Victorian-era aesthetics.

Beside the hotel is Amsterdam's premier department store, the **Bijenkorf** (Dam 1), to which you might want to return at a later time. Also on this side of the square is the somewhat insipid (or understated) **Nationaal Monument ➊**, a 22-metre (72ft) high obelisk commemorating Holland's liberation from German occupation in World War II. Cross the busy street that bisects the Dam, to the **Koninklijk Paleis**

The Dam, one of the city's main squares.

(Royal Palace; www.paleisamsterdam. nl; daily 10am–5pm, closed during royal events). Constructed by Jacob van Campen between 1648 and 1655, the building served as the town hall, until Napoleon Bonaparte's younger brother Louis was appointed king of the Netherlands and took it for his palace in 1808. The Royal Palace compensates for its rather heavy-handed neoclassical exterior with an elegant interior that brims with white marble.

CHURCH OF CORONATIONS

More interesting might be an exhibition at the neo-Gothic **Nieuwe Kerk** (New Church), the Netherlands' state church, which, when monarchs are not being crowned, is mostly used as an exhibition space and recital venue (it has two superb 16th- and 17th-century organs). Famous Dutch figures such as the 17th-century admiral Michiel de Ruyter, as well as the poet and playwright Joost

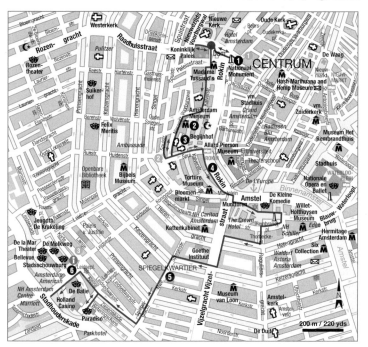

The Begijnhof.

van den Vondel, are buried here. The final point of interest in the Dam neighbourhood is **Madame Tussauds** (20 Dam; www.madametussauds.com/amsterdam; daily 10am–8pm but with many seasonal changes, check website). Featured among the waxworks museum's models are Dutch personalities such as Rembrandt and Mata Hari, and a cast of international big names such as Churchill and Gandhi.

THE AMSTERDAM MUSEUM

For some more background history, head along Kalverstraat, Amsterdam's popular pedestrians-only shopping street, to the **Amsterdam Museum ❷** (Kalverstraat 92 and Nieuwezijds Voorburgwal 357; www.amsterdam museum.nl; daily 10am–5pm). The museum takes visitors on a trip through the centuries, illustrating Amsterdam's transformation from a muddy medieval fishing village, through the expansive sea power of the Golden Age, to today's sophisticated metropolis. The museum is housed in a 16th-century orphanage.

If you are ready for lunch at this point, leave through the museum's Nieuwezijds Voorburgwal exit, walk a short distance to Spui then take a right into **Spuistraat**. Here, at No. 24, you will find the **Café Luxembourg**, see ❷. Although in some people's opinion a tad pretentious, it serves good food – many of its dishes are specialities taken from the menus of well-regarded restaurants and cafés in the city.

BROWSING THROUGH BOOKS

After lunch you should be ready for **Spui**. On one corner you will find the **Athenaeum News Centre**, which has a good range of international titles. Outside is **'t Lieverdje** (Little Darling), a bronze sculpture of a boy standing with hands on hips and grinning broadly at passers-by. Every Friday there is a good second-hand book market in Spui, and a Sunday art market from March to September. Waterstone's, the British bookshop chain, has a branch on the square, although the entrance is at Kalverstraat 152. Also superb for books is the **American Book Center**, at Spui 12 (Mon noon–8pm, Tue–Sat 10am–8pm, Sun 11am–6.30pm).

BEGIJNHOF

If you walk down Spui to Nos 10–17, you will reach the **Begijnhof ❸** (daily 8am–5pm; free). This beautiful, tranquil courtyard dates from 1346 and for centuries was the home of pious, unmarried Catholic laywomen (*begijns*) who lived a semi-monastic life in the service of the community. The last *begijn* died in 1970. The Begijnhof's little gabled houses, built between the 14th and 17th centuries are now the homes of elderly retired women – try not to disturb them. In spring the Begijnhof lawn's carpet of daffodils and crocuses complements the spiritual atmosphere. The Begijnhof's 17th-century Presbyterian church was originally

Tuschinski Theater.   *Rembrandtplein.*

Catholic – the *begijns* were compelled to hand it over after the triumph of Calvinism in Amsterdam. Across the lawn, **Het Houten Huys** (The Wooden House) at No. 34 dates from 1425. It is the city's oldest house and one of only two remaining wooden residences; the other one is 't Aepjen (see page 45).

Walk along Spui to **Rokin** ❹, where you will see the canal-boat moorings of the Rederij P Kooij ferry company. Here too is the traditional cigar-and-pipe shop **P G C Hajenius** (Nos 92–6), whose humidors are world-renowned. Continue along Rokin to Muntplein (see route 1), then across to Reguliersbreestraat. At a later date you might want to take in a movie at the startlingly Art Deco **Tuschinski Theater** at Nos 26–28; in the meantime, take a turn around its magnificent lobby.

REMBRANDTPLEIN

If you didn't have lunch, try a falafel at **Falafel Koning** in Regulierssteeg, opposite the Tuschinski – take it away to eat over a great view: the bridge over the Binnenamstel, at the point where the River Amstel runs into the city and its maze of canals. Continue into **Rembrandtplein** and check out the undistinguished statue of Rembrandt in the little garden at its centre. Busy, brassy Rembrandtplein is full of mediocre-to-average cafés, where aspiring musicians play in the evening. If you're looking for quality, try the **Café De Kroon** at No. 17

(see route 14), which has an excellent enclosed balcony that overlooks the square; alternatively, at Nos 26–36, is **Café Schiller**, the wood-panelled bar of the Hotel NH Schiller (see route 14).

ART AND ANTIQUES

Leave the square by Thorbeckeplein. If you're passing this way on a Sunday afternoon (between March and December), you will pass through the street stalls of the **Thorbeckeplein Art Market**, a sophisticated little gathering that sits somewhat incongruously beside the topless bars in this small, handsome square. Then take Herengracht, Vijzelstraat and Keizersgracht. There isn't a good way to do this by public transport, and you must at least partially retrace a section of route 1 (see page 26) to Nieuwe Spiegelstraat and its extension along Spiegelgracht.

You are now in the **Spiegelkwartier** antiques district ❺, where antiques shops are thickly clustered along the narrow street and the pretty canal. Look out for the wonderfully old-fashioned toy shop, **Tinkerbell**, at Spiegelgracht 10. Not only do none of the toys bleep, whirr or zap, but a good many are actually made of wood.

Emerging from the antiques district into **Kleine Lijnbaansgracht**, turn right past a higgledy-piggledy row of canal houses, and a parade of restaurants, to **Leidseplein** ❻. In the summer this district comes into its own as a centre of

Café terrace on Leidseplein.

entertainment. In addition to the cafés, restaurants, theatres, cinemas and clubs, there is any number of diverse street performers, typically fire-eaters and buskers (see also route 13). As you stroll around the square, soaking up the atmosphere, remember to be wary of pickpockets.

CAFÉS FOR PEOPLE-WATCHING

Leidseplein's cafés are good for people-watching. Particularly recommended is **Reynders**, see ③. Despite being in such a touristy location, it retains elements of old-world, brown-café charm, and it has a cosy, glassed-in terrace. A good choice for afternoon tea is the Café Américain in the American Hotel (a fine example of Art Nouveau) at Leidsekade 97.

Although by now it will be quite late in the day, there may still be people playing chess with huge plastic pieces at **Max Euweplein**, a satellite of Leidseplein. Other attractions in the area include the **Holland Casino Amsterdam**, the mooring of Rederij Noord-Zuid (a canal-boat company) and, in and around Leidseplein, several cinemas.

Among the enormous choice of eateries in this neighbourhood, you could opt to dine at the excellent seafood restaurant, **De Oesterbar**, at Leidseplein 10. After that, if you're still wide awake and suitably dressed, you may want to try your luck at the casino on Max Euweplein.

Food and Drink

① GRAND HOTEL KRASNAPOLSKY

Dam 9; tel: 020-554 6114; www.nh-hotels.nl/hotel/nh-amsterdam-grand-hotel-krasnapolsky; breakfast Mon–Sat 6.30–11am, Sun 6.30am–noon; €€
The Krasnapolsky is one of the grandest of the city's grand hotels and the buffet breakfast here is chance to see the ornate decor of the 1855 building without breaking the bank. There's also a children's breakfast menu.

② CAFÉ LUXEMBOURG

Spuistraat 24; tel: 020-620 6264; www.cafeluxembourg.amsterdam; Sun–Thu 9am–midnight, Fri–Sat 9am–1am; €€
The Café Luxembourg has earned its place as one of the smartest restaurants in Amsterdam. An unusual feature of its menu is that it includes a number of dishes inspired by some of the city's other favourite eating places.

③ CAFÉ REYNDERS

Leidsestraat 6; tel: 020-623 4419; www.cafereynders.nl; daily 9am–2am; €€
Another celebrated brown café, the Reynders is a youngster having only opened in 1896. They serve simple but good dishes like baked salmon and cottage pie, and have a huge list of *jenevers* as well as other spirits, beer and wine.

The Rijksmuseum.

THE MUSEUM QUARTER

This itinerary focuses on the city's most important museums: the Rijksmuseum, the Van Gogh Museum, and the Stedelijk Museum. The route also takes in the Concertgebouw concert hall, two of the city's premier shopping streets, and Vondelpark.

DISTANCE: 2km (1.2 miles)
TIME: a full day, if visiting all the museums
START: Rijksmuseum
END: Vondelpark
POINTS TO NOTE: You can do this walk any day as all three of Amsterdam's main art museums are open daily. Try to be at the Rijksmuseum for 9am. If there are long queues for the Van Gogh Museum, skip it now and go back early another day.

For art lovers Amsterdam is a huge draw, as its museums – three of them conveniently next to each other in the Museum Quarter – have unique appeal. The biggest collections of work by two of the world's greatest artists are held here: Rembrandt and Vincent Van Gogh. Rembrandt spent much of his life here, and the Rijksmuseum holds an impressive collection of his work. By contrast, Van Gogh spent very little time here, and didn't much enjoy it either, but the Van Gogh Museum's unrivalled collection means his name is now forever associated with the city. Those two museums, and the Stedelijk Museum which covers modern art, have all been impressively refurbished in recent years, making them a joy to visit.

Start on Jan Luijkenstraat at the entrance to the Rijksmuseum, one stop east of Leidseplein by the No. 2 or 5 tram. These museums are so outstanding that, even if it happens to be a beautiful day, you might choose to sacrifice the sunshine for some high culture. Even if you know nothing of art, you will probably appreciate the offerings within their stately walls.

THE RIJKSMUSEUM

The dominant building on Museumplein is the palatial **Rijksmuseum** ❶ (www.rijksmuseum.nl; daily 9am–5pm), the most important museum in the Netherlands. It is housed in a grand late-19th century building which was opened in 1885 and designed by the same man who produced the Centraal Station,

Vermeer's The Milkmaid.

Petrus Josephus Hubertus Cuypers. Because of its venerable age it had long been due for a refurbishment, and after a period of ten years when it was partly closed, it re-opened again fully in 2013. One of the features of the new museum is a state-of-the-art lighting system, using 750,000 LED lights to simulate natural daylight.

The highlight is still the separate room in which the single-most important work in the Rijksmuseum, Rembrandt's *The Night Watch*, is displayed to great effect. Among other highlights on display are exquisitely detailed 17th-century dolls' houses, fully 'furnished', with tiny Delftware plates, paintings, copper plates, and precious silver, glass and porcelain objects, most of which were made by respected craftsmen. Comparable to the richly decorated cabinets of collectors, these dolls' houses were not made as playthings for children but for women of the regent and merchant classes. In addition, there is a beautiful collection of Delftware, with delightful pieces, such as a polychrome pair of pointed, high-heeled shoes and a violin, among the more familiar jugs and plates.

The Night Watch

Start with the foremost attraction, Rembrandt's *The Night Watch*. Painted in 1642, this group portrait of a colourfully attired militia company has come to represent not only Rembrandt but the entire Dutch Golden Age. Its iconic status might not be immediately apparent – don't be surprised if, like many visitors, you are far from overwhelmed at first sight. The militiamen themselves hated the picture and their hostile reception sent Rembrandt into a tailspin that led to bankruptcy. Yet it is a magnificent spectacle when viewed as a whole, a tour de force of colour, light and composition. Up close you can focus on the individual faces (including Rembrandt's own), which express the confidence and pride of a young nation that had liberated itself from the Spanish colonial yoke and saw an exciting new world opening up before it. Be prepared for some queuing if you want to see the work from a good vantage point.

A host of other great paintings by the Dutch masters hang on nearby walls. Johannes (Jan) Vermeer is well represented, and his effective use of light can be seen in *The Milkmaid* (c.1658–60) and *Woman Reading a Letter* (c.1663), two of the gallery's best-loved pieces.

There are paintings by Frans Hals, the founding artist of the Dutch School, along with landscapes by Jacob van Ruisdael, bawdy escapades by Jan Steen, and artists influenced by the masters.

MUSEUMPLEIN

Leave the Rijksmuseum on Museumstraat, which cuts across **Museumplein**. Grassy areas extend uninterrupted

Museumplein.   *Rembrandt's The Night Watch.*

across the square, creating a grand promenade and affording a pleasant refuge for relaxation, while making its cultural citadels easily accessible. There is a separate area for sport and play, and a bicycle path. Colourful benches and stylish lanterns have been dotted across the area. Skateboarders have their terrain on one side and boules and basketball players on the other. Across from the Rijksmuseum, the **Cobra Café**, see ❶, pays homage to the COBRA art movement; its outdoor terrace can seat nearly 200. Just beside it a long pond freezes in winter to become an ice-skating rink. Nearby, the Van Gogh Museum and Rijksmuseum share a gift-shop pavilion selling posters, cards and souvenirs relating to their collections.

CONCERTGEBOUW

Walk to the end of Museumplein, to **Van Baerlestraat** and the **Concertgebouw** ❷ (Concert Building; Concertgebouwplein 2–6; www.con

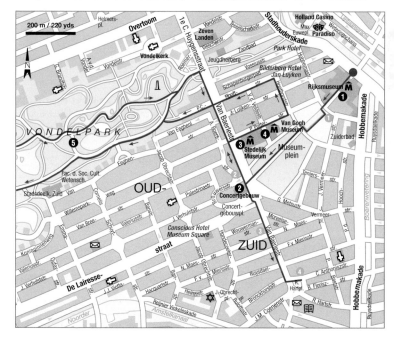

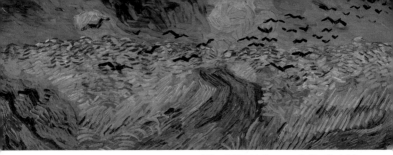

Wheatfield with Crows at the Van Gogh Museum.

certgebouw.nl). Built in 1887 by the architect A.L. van Gendt, this is one of the world's great classical music halls and the home of the Concertgebouw Orchestra. A golden lyre stands on the roof above the entrance, and the neoclassical colonnade is watched over by severe portrait busts of Beethoven, Sweelinck and Bach. Among the composers who have held court here are Brahms, Stravinsky, Strauss and Mahler. If you are here on a Wednesday around lunchtime, you may be able to listen to the orchestra rehearsing for free. Or you might want to buy tickets for an evening concert.

There is an excellent restaurant next door to the Concertgebouw, **Brasserie Keyzer**, see ②, where, in a much recounted incident, a musician from the Concertgebouw Orchestra was once mistaken for a waiter. Or you could walk south along Van Baerlestraat to **De Knijp**, see ③, which is equally good and less stuffy. For what might be the best option of all, walk a little further, to Roelof Hartplein, for lunch in the chic café-restaurant **De Wildschuut**, which has a pavement terrace, see ④.

Rijksmuseum Reborn

The reopening of the Rijksmuseum after a 10-year closure was a lavish affair with processions, bands, dramatic fireworks engulfing the building and great crowds flocking to see Queen Beatrix. The opening was the Queen's last official duty before abdication when she turned the throne over to her son, Willem-Alexander, declaring that the future of the nation 'lies with the next generation'. Interestingly, her gala abdication dinner was held, not in the Royal Palace, but in the Gallery of Honour in the newly restored Rijksmuseum.

Restoration took 10 years instead of the intended five, due largely to the lengthy battle with the powerful Dutch cycling lobby who objected to the proposed closure of the cycle thoroughfare which runs smack through the museum, separating the two courtyards. The cyclists triumphed, their route was retained and the architects came up with an ingenious solution of digging down 5 metres (3ft), using boats and divers, to create the atrium, finally linking the two courtyards.

MODERN ART

After lunch, retrace your steps along Van Baerlestraat, passing the Concertgebouw, to the **Stedelijk Museum** ⑤ (13 Paulus Potterstraat 13; www.stedelijk.nl; Sat–Thu 10am–6pm, Fri until 10pm). The Stedelijk stretches the definition of modern art back to the mid-19th century, finishing at the end of the 20th century. It has an incredible collection of non-Dutch masters, including works by Braque, Breitner, Calder, Cézanne, Chagall, Israëls, Kandinsky, Malevich, Manet, Matisse, Monet, Old-

The Stedelijk Museum.

enburg, Picasso, Renoir, Rosenquist and Warhol. The Dutch collection is outstanding, particularly the Appel collection where there are De Koonings and Mondrians on display.

VAN GOGH MUSEUM

The last of the big three museums, the **Van Gogh Museum** ❹ (Museumplein 6; www.vangoghmuseum.nl; Sat–Thu 9am–6pm, Fri until 9pm) may be the highlight of your visit to Amsterdam. Vincent Van Gogh (1853–90) is the subject of passionate devotion throughout the world, and his paintings command astronomical prices at auction. This is particularly ironic considering the poverty and lack of recognition suffered by the artist in his short lifetime. The museum contains some 200 Van Gogh paintings – including *The Potato Eaters* and *Sunflowers* – and 500 of his drawings, along with the artist's collection of Japanese wood carvings. The library of letters features examples of the correspondence between Vincent and his brother Theo. The museum also displays works by Toulouse-Lautrec, Gauguin and other major international artists.

Van Gogh's paintings are arranged in simple chronological order, which makes it easy to trace his development as an artist from the darkly foreboding works of his early Dutch and Belgian period, through the burgeoning of colour in Paris, to the luminous, swirling masterpieces he painted in the clear light of Provence. There is an inevitable question mark at the end of this sequence: what more would he have achieved and what recognition might he have received if he had not cut short his own life at the age of 37? Temporary exhibitions are displayed at the ellipse-shaped, partially subterranean wing designed by the Japanese architect Kisho Kurokawa.

DESIGNER CLOTHES

Having had your fill of museums you might be in the mood for some shopping in Van Baerlestraat and the adjoining **Pieter Cornelisz Hooftstraat** (which is generally shortened to PC Hooftstraat, or 'the PC Hooft'), two blocks down Van Baerlestraat from the Stedelijk Museum. These are Amsterdam's two top-rated shopping streets and it makes sense to take advantage of being in the area. Lots of smart and trendy designer-clothes outlets are located here, particularly in the PC Hooft.

VONDELPARK

On long summer evenings, you could take in the city's atmosphere by walking to the western end of PC Hooftstraat for a leisurely stroll in **Vondelpark** ❺, named after the poet and playwright Joost van den Von-

An ornate bridge in Vondelpark.

del (1587–1689). After dark this is not such a sensible option because the park becomes less attractive and less safe. The park serves as both garden and playground. In typical Dutch fashion, Vondelpark has lots of water, in the shape of long, sinuous pools around which crowds gather to sunbathe in summer. In addition to the park's usual activities – walking, cycling, jogging, frisbee-throwing, and ice-cream guzzling – one of the most enjoyable pursuits, for the young at heart at least, is roller-blading. Rent a pair of roller-blades (and protective gear) from a skate rental at the Amstelveenseweg end of the park and, kitted out like an imperial stormtrooper from *Star Wars*, you can power-blade (or power-stumble) around the expanses of Vondelpark.

For dinner you could return to Van Baerlestraat and the **Brasserie Keyzer** – be sure to order your meal from a waiter and not from the lead violin – or to **De Knijp**.

Food and Drink

① COBRA CAFÉ

Hobbemastraat 18; tel: 020-470 0111; www.cobracafe.nl; daily 9.30am–7pm; €
This modern café is open for lunch through till the early evening, and has two outdoor terraces. Dishes include salads, sandwiches, pizzas, pies and a few other hot dishes, with soft and alcoholic drinks also on offer.

② BRASSERIE KEYZER

Van Baerlestraat 96; tel: 020-675 1866; http://brasseriekeyzer.nl; daily 10am–11pm; €€
Ideally located for the Concertgebouw, the Brasserie Keyzer has been serving fine cuisine since 1903, and counts classical musicians and conductors among its regulars. There are seasonal fixed-price menus as well as à la carte and a banqueting menu.

③ DE KNIJP

Van Baerlestraat 134; tel: 020-671 4248; www.deknijp.nl; daily 5.30pm–12.30am; €€
What began as a pub in 1974 is now also a restaurant serving inexpensive but good food, including Zeeland oysters, home-made pâté and home-smoked salmon, with an additional lunch menu and a small but affordable wine list.

④ DE WILDSCHUUT

Roelof Hartplein 1–3; tel: 020-676 8220; http://cafewildschut.nl; Mon–Fri 9am–late, Sat–Şun 10am–late; €€
This permanently fashionable café-restaurant has a pavement terrace that is good for catching some late-afternoon sunshine, which might explain its popularity with after-hours office workers. The food ranges from simple bar snacks to well-prepared international dishes.

The Oude Kerk.

THE OLD CENTRE (THE WALLEN)

Take a leisurely stroll through the infamous Rosse Buurt (red-light district) in daylight hours, when you can appreciate the many non-erotic attractions of this beautiful old part of Amsterdam.

DISTANCE: 2km (1.2 miles)
TIME: 2 hours
START: Grand Hotel Krasnapolsky, The Dam
END: De Waag
POINTS TO NOTE: If you want to see inside the Oude Kerk, note that it's closed on Sunday mornings unless you're attending a service. If travelling with children, note that this walk does take you through the red-light district.

One of the peculiarities of the red-light district is that, being so central, it exists side-by-side with churches and other old buildings of historic significance. You needn't be put off seeing these because of the location, and you can enjoy the Old Town during the day without having to see quite so much of the oldest profession, if that's what you prefer. It would be a shame, after all, to miss the chance to see one of only two wooden houses left in the city, as well as attractions like the world's oldest stock exchange and one of Amster-

dam's most impressive churches. But to remind you where you are, there are also the Erotic Museum and the Hash Marihuana and Hemp Museum!

Start at the Dam outside the Grand Hotel Krasnapolsky, or inside if you want breakfast at the coffee bar.

THE OLD STOCK EXCHANGE

Walk along Damrak in the direction of Centraal Station, and turn right into Beursplein. Here, in addition to the fountain and tree-shaded benches, you will find the early-20th-century **Beurs van Berlage** ❶ (Beursplein 1; www.beursvanberlage.nl; Mon–Fri 9am–5pm, event and exhibition opening times vary). This, the old Stock Exchange, is now a museum, exhibition hall and concert venue. In its main hall you can admire the plain ironwork, narrow arcades, and Romanesque and neo-Renaissance motifs.

Take Beursstraat, then turn right onto Paternostersteeg, and continue through Wijde Kerksteeg to Oudekerk-splein. (If by chance Paternostersteeg is

The pretty interior of the Oude Kerk.

closed, continue on to Oude Brugsteeg, turn right into Warmoesstraat, and then left into Wijde Kerksteeg for Oudekerk-splein.) The foundations of the **Oude Kerk ❷** (Old Church; www.oudekerk.nl; Mon–Sat 10am–6pm, Sun 1–5.30pm) were laid in 1300, but the triple-naved church was not completed until 1577. A walk around the tree-shaded square gives a good impression of the red-light district: the venerable old church, pretty canal and gabled houses now seem rather incongruous amid the prostitutes' parlours and sex clubs.

THE GRAND

Walk along the **Oudezijds Voorburgwal** canal, past more red-fringed rooms and a couple of good sec-ond-hand bookshops. The 17th- and 18th-cen-tury houses at Nos 101–7, 133–5 and 232 have interestingly-shaped gables. Across Damstraat, still on Oudezijds Voor-burgwal, the character of the area changes to one of handsome houses and offices in the old gabled canal-side buildings. At No. 197 is **The Grand ❸**, one of Amsterdam's swankiest hotels, officially known as the Hotel Sofitel Legend the Grand Amster-

dam. Located in a 16th-century building that was once the **Prinsenhof** (Royal Inn), it's well worth entering for a look. At No. 231 the **Athenaeum Illustre**, dat-ing from 1632, was the forerunner of the University of Amsterdam, whose campus you are now entering.

Turn left into Grimburgwal, noting the scenic junction of three canals at this point (the 17th-century house at the intersection has been dubbed the Huis aan de Drie Grachten, or House on the Three Canals). Walk to the far side

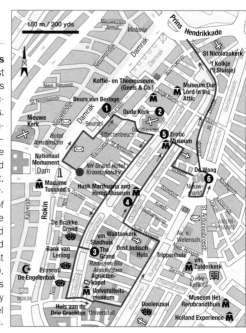

The Athenaeum Illustre.   *De Waag.*

of Oudezijds Achterburgwal, then right into Oudemanhuispoort, an arcade that hosts an excellent second-hand book market. Midway along the arcade, on the left, automatic doors open onto a garden courtyard. Turning left at the end of the arcade, you enter Kloveniersburgwal, passing the **Oost-Indisch Huis** (East India House), which was once the headquarters of the United East India Company and which now houses university offices. Its main entrance is on **Oude Hoogstraat**, leading back to Oudezijds Achterburgwal.

MARIHUANA MUSEUM

Located on the far side of the canal are two museums that bring a touch of what you might call culture (if you're willing to stretch the term) to the red-light district. First up is the **Hash Marihuana and Hemp Museum** ❹ (Oudezijds Achterburgwal 130; http://hashmuseum.com; daily 10am–10pm). This could be described as an 'educational' experience. Amsterdam and the noxious weed are all but synonymous, and here you get the lowdown on the high. In fact, the museum is extremely well placed – this area is the centre of street drug-dealing in the city.

Then there is the **Erotic Museum** ❺ (Oudezijds Achterburgwal 54; www.erotisch-museum.nl; Sun–Thu 11am–1am, Fri–Sat until 2am), which is more about decorations of a bawdy nature. It treats its subject matter seriously, and includes 19th-century photographs

showing Victorians being far from prim and proper. Above the entrance is a gable stone dating from 1685; it is decorated with a castle motif and proclaims, in the words of Martin Luther, *"God is myn burgh"* (God is my stronghold).

Cross the canal bridge and return along the canal for a short distance to Bloedstraat, then into **Nieuwmarkt**. The 14th-century **De Waag** ❻ on the square was one of the city's fortified gates. Now it is a multimedia centre with a wonderful, atmospheric restaurant, **In den Waag**, see ❶. Nearby is Zeedijk, which was once a 'shooting gallery' for Amsterdam's heroin addicts. Now cleaned up, it is a fairly attractive shopping street that curves into a restaurants-and-bars zone before ending opposite Centraal Station. At No. 1 is **'t Aepjen**, a wooden house dating from 1550, one of only two such houses left in the city (the 15th-century Het Houten Huys is located near the Begijnhof (see page 35).

Hortus Botanicus.

THE ZOO DISTRICT

This half-day trip takes in the Botanical Gardens, The Artis Royal Zoo and the Tropenmuseum (Tropical Museum).

DISTANCE: 2km (1.2 miles)
TIME: Half-day, or longer with visits to attractions
START/END: Waterlooplein
POINTS TO NOTE: This is a good walk for families, as it can include visits to the zoo and to the Tropenmuseum Junior, aimed specifically at kids.

This eastern part of the city gets slightly fewer visitors than the centre and the Museum Quarter, which is a shame as it's easy to get to. The first of its main sights, the Hortus Botanicus, is just across the Herengracht canal from Waterlooplein, with the city's zoo a short walk away, and another of Amsterdam's fascinating museum, the Tropenmuseum, a few minutes beyond that.

This is the Plantage district of the city, the name meaning Plantation, which is appropriate as it has a much greener and more open feel than the city centre. It became part of Amsterdam in 1663, and then in 1682 the Botanical Gardens moved here from its original location. The

area was once the centre of Amsterdam's diamond industry, and some of the old factory buildings remain, but it is largely still a residential district and a pleasant place to stroll around. Start at Waterlooplein, which is served by tram line 14 as well as the metro to Waterlooplein station.

HORTUS BOTANICUS

Either walk across Mr Visserplein to Muiderstraat, or hop on tram 14 for one stop. (We revisit Waterlooplein on Route 11: The Jewish Quarter, see page 63, so you may not want to linger there now.) Cross the bridge over Nieuwe Herengracht and you will see **Hortus Botanicus** ❶ (Botanical Garden; Plantage Middenlaan 2a; www.dehortus.nl; daily 10am–5pm, Sun July–Aug until 7pm) on your right.

Founded in 1638 as the Hortus Medicus, the Botanical Garden is one of the world's oldest. It moved to its present location in 1682. With some 250,000 flowers and 115,000 plants and trees, including 4,000 different varieties, the garden is a medley of colour and scent, and a relaxing place for a stroll. It owes much to the

Lions at Artis Royal Zoo.   A bird display at the zoo.

treasure trove of tropical plants the Dutch found in their former colonies of Indonesia, Surinam and the Antilles, and not a little of its popularity to the national infatuation with flowers – not only tulips.

Among the garden's highlights are the **Semicircle** behind the entrance – a reconstruction of part of the original layout from 1682; the **Butterfly House**; the **Palm House**, comprising one of the world's oldest collection of palm trees;

and the **Three-Climate House**, grouping tropical, subtropical and desert plants, with a gallery that simulates the atmosphere of a jungle. You can get a snack from the **Oranjerie** (see ❶), or you might want to check out the shop's souvenirs.

ARTIS ROYAL ZOO

Walk or take tram No 14 one stop along Plantage Middenlaan to **Artis Royal**

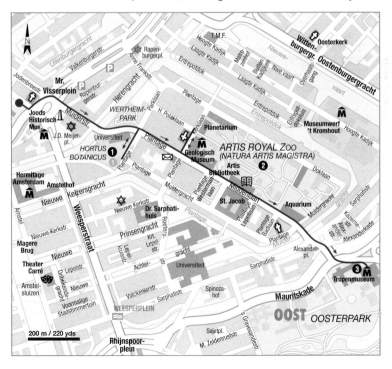

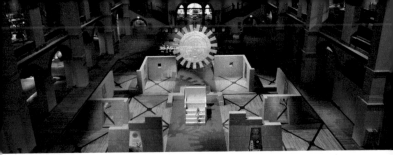

Inside the Tropenmuseum.

Zoo ❷ (Plantage Kerklaan 38–40; www. artis.nl; daily Mar–Oct 9am–6pm, Nov–Feb 9am–5pm, June–Aug until sundown on Sat) – the country's oldest. Like zoos throughout the world, Artis has made a big effort to replace the cruel exploitation of animals with a facility that promotes the appreciation and preservation of the natural world's living creatures, with a particular emphasis placed on authenticity. The African Savannah, for instance, consists of a micro-plain that is home to zebras, wildebeest, ostriches and other birds. Artis, which has been open since 1838, does its best in this respect, but the animals don't have much space. Regardless, the zoo is an enormous attraction, particularly for children.

The range of animals includes tigers, leopards, elephants, camels, polar bears, gorillas, peacocks, seals and so forth. There is in addition an aviary, a reptile house, a nocturnal house, a **Planetarium** (closed Mon am) and a **Geological Museum**. The zoo's garden layout and range of tree and plant species rival those of the Hortus Botanicus. The **Aquarium** is well presented, particularly the sections on the River Amazon, coral reefs, and Amsterdam's own canals, with their fish populations and urban detritus.

TROPENMUSEUM

Continue along Plantage Middenlaan, either on foot or for two stops on the No. 14 tram, to the **Tropenmuseum ❸** (Tropical Museum; Linnaeusstraat 2; www.tropenmuseum.nl; Tue–Sun 10am–5pm, July–Aug also Mon). As at the Hortus Botanicus, the impetus behind the Tropenmuseum came from the Dutch colonies in the tropics. The extravagant building says a lot about the European colonial ideal. This is not to suggest that the museum is a dusty monument to vanished glory; it is a highly relevant evocation of life and environment in the tropics, with emphasis on the threats posed by burgeoning populations and ecological destruction. If you are travelling with youngsters, you could take them to the **Kindermuseum**. It is designed for children, though of course adults are allowed, so long as they are in the guise of chaperones. Once you have had your fill of flora and fauna, you can take the No. 14 tram back to Waterlooplein.

Food and Drink

❶ ORANJERIE

Hortus Botanicus Amsterdam, Plantage Middenlaan 2a; tel: 020-702 5405; www. dehortus.nl/bezoek/the-hortus-store-cafe; daily 10am–5pm; €
The 1875 Oranjerie at the Hortus Botanicus is one of the most delightful places to eat in Amsterdam. You dine here surrounded by plants. They offer a simple coffee and pastry breakfast, or a fixed-price three-course lunch with a glass of wine.

Centraal Station.

THE HARBOUR

The harbour itinerary covers the 'little islands' at one end and the Maritime Museum at the other, and includes an optional two-minute 'cruise' on the IJ ferry to Amsterdam North.

DISTANCE: 6.5km (4 miles)
TIME: 4 hours
START: Centraal Station
END: NEMO Science Centre
POINTS TO NOTE: As you will be using public transport for part of the itinerary, make sure you have an electronic OV-chipkaart (see page 120).

Docks and harbours aren't always the most interesting part of a city, but Amsterdam's is an exception. The city was effectively built on water – many of its streets are actually filled-in canals, and water flows under the city in places, not always visible. Walk out of Centraal Station and you face the city, and it's easy to forget the vast amount of water behind the station, and to either side.

The harbour area is constantly changing, and being redeveloped. In 1997 the remarkable futuristic building housing the NEMO Science Centre opened, and the Scheepvaartmuseum is housed in what used to be a naval warehouse. More recently the EYE Film Institute relocated

to an appropriately eye-catching building, across the water from Centraal Station and just outside the scope of this walk, but you can take the free *Buiksloterweg* ferry from behind the station to get there.

CENTRAAL STATION

It's well worth taking the time to have a good look at **Centraal Station**. Constructed on an artificial island in the IJ channel, the station opened in 1895 and was heartily disliked at the time. Today the station is a tourist attraction in its own right, partly for its extravagant architecture and partly for the lively atmosphere that surrounds it. Street musicians, particularly traditional barrel-organ grinders, for some reason, line up to perform here. Nine of the city's 14 tram routes begin and end their journeys at Centraal Station, as do three of the five metro lines, and a number of bus routes.

Two VVV (local tourism) centres – one inside and the other outside the station – dispense information and book hotel rooms for tourists. If you haven't had breakfast or you want a coffee, the **1e**

NEMO and the replica of the Amsterdam.

Klas buffet on platform one is excellent.

There are enough bicycles chained up in this area to constitute an obstacle to navigation. The Museum Line boats also stop at the station. A note of warning – beware of pickpockets in this area.

RIVER TRAFFIC

Now it is time to hit the water. For a good view of Amsterdam harbour, take one or both of the ferries that cross the IJ channel from a pier ❶ at the rear of Centraal Station. Unusually for Amsterdam, the shortest ferry trips are free. The **Buiksloterweg** is a covered landing craft that crosses the channel in two minutes, while another ferry takes five minutes for its crossing to a point further east. Both vessels will transport your bicycle (or other two-wheeled vehicles).

On the way across the busy channel you will probably intersect the wakes of canal boats and pleasure boats, and perhaps a visiting warship or cruise liner. Watch out for the Royal Dutch Shell office tower on the north bank – its windows are laced with gold dust and sparkle in the sunlight.

There is not a great deal to see in Amsterdam North, which is mostly a modern residential area, and you probably won't want to spend much time on the north bank. Ferries come and go every few minutes, so you should not have very long to wait before returning to Centraal Station.

Walk or take the No. 48 bus from the stop outside Centraal Station on De Rui-

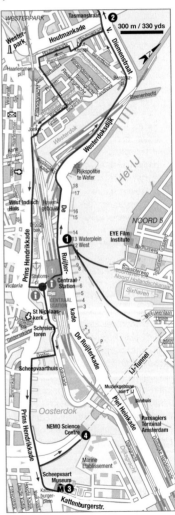

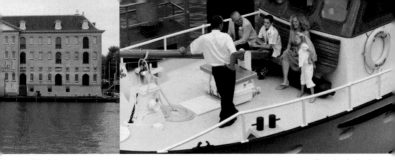

The Scheepvaartmuseum.   *Boat in the harbour.*

jterkade (beside the Holland International canal-boat jetty) to **Tasmanstraat** ❷ to experience the old harbour's ambience. On the left side of Tasmanstraat is a cramped area – full of characterful warehouses, docks, small boatyards and other harbour installations – that is being converted into residences.

Take a stroll down Houtmankade, passing the children's playground on Zoutkeetsplein, until you reach the end of Houtmankade, then turn left onto Schiemanstraat and Sloterdijkstraat. Walk across the narrow bridge over Prinseneilandsgracht, to Galgenstraat and Kleine Bickersstraat.

SCHEEPVAART MUSEUM

Take the No. 22 bus back to Centraal Station for lunch at the station buffet or the more formal **1e Klas** restaurant on Platform 2B, see ❶, before heading by foot to Kattenburgerplein. Alternatively, stay on the bus and continue to Kattenburgerplein and cross to the **Scheepvaart Museum** ❸ (Maritime Museum; Kattenburgerplein 1; www.hetscheepvaartmuseum.nl; daily 9am–5pm). Housed in the former Amsterdam Admiralty building, dating from 1656, the museum documents and celebrates Holland's seafaring history, with a pronounced emphasis on the 17th century, when the country was one of the world's great sea powers.

A full-scale replica of the 17th-century Dutch East Indiaman, the *Amsterdam*, is moored to a jetty outside the museum. It presents a fantastic sight, a squat yet elegant mountain of timber surmounted by three tall masts and threaded with a tracery of rigging. Breezes from the nearby shipping channel roil the water and set the *Amsterdam* swaying gently at her moorings.

NEMO

Follow the waterfront around Kattenburgerplein, past a sculpture of Amphitrite (the wife of the Greek God of the Seas, Poseidon), to the long stairway that leads up to the wonderful, and child-friendly, **NEMO Science Centre** ❹ (Oosterdok 2; www.nemosciencemuseum.nl; mid-Feb–early Sept and school holidays daily 10am–5.30pm, early Sept–mid-Feb Tue–Sun 10am–5.30pm). Like its many interactive exhibits, the centre's futuristic architecture reflects the high-tech experience of life in the 21st century.

The Stromma canal cruise ticket booth.

THE CANALS BY PEDAL BIKE

*Take your own mini–cruise, riding a water pedal bike along the canals,
and get a better feeling for life in Amsterdam.*

TIME: 1.5 hours
START/END: Anne Frank Huis
POINTS TO NOTE: You can rent a pedal
bike for either 1 or 1.5 hours, and
children must be at least 4 years old.

Amsterdam's canals go back to the Golden
Age of the 17th century and the city owes
its look and shape and very existence to
these man-made channels. People cross
them every day and many people live on
them in house-boats. Amsterdammers
look down their noses at water-bikes, but
tourists seem to love them. Amsterdam is
best seen from the water, and as captain
of a two- or four-person water bike you'll
get a different perspective on the city.

For information, contact **Stromma**
(www.stromma.nl) who have a mooring on
Prinsengracht ❶, next to the Anne Frank
Huis. (They also have moorings at Leidseplein and the Rijksmuseum, and you
can hire and return bikes at any of them.)
You will be told the rules when you hire a
water-bike: you cannot sail on the IJ channel or the River Amstel, and there may
be other places that are out of bounds.
The canals can get busy, so watch out
for potential problems, particularly when
passing under bridges. In bad weather,
the bikes, which are safe and unsinkable,
can be fitted with rain shields.

Food and Drink

❶ BISTRO BIJ ONS

Prinsengracht 287; tel: 020-627 9016;
www.bistrobijons.nl; Tue–Sun 10am–
midnight; €€
This cosy place in the Jordaan combines
the feel of a brown café with a French
bistro. It serves traditional Dutch fare with
names like granny's casserole and mom's
stewed beef, and they also have a good
selection of Dutch liqueurs.

SIDE-CANALS

Pedal southwards along Prinsengracht,
past Lauriergracht, Looiersgracht and
then Passeerdersgracht. Take the opportunity to turn into one or more of these

Pedalling down the canal.

Take care when passing under bridges.

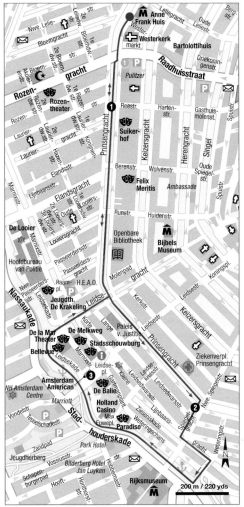

side canals, which are quiet but interesting. At Leidsegracht, you can turn off, but it's better to plough straight ahead, under Leidsestraat, until you reach the pretty **Spiegelgracht ❷**, where you should turn right. Continue to the end then turn left under the bridge into Lijnbaansgracht.

Turn right after the **Café Mankind** at the first corner on the right to a short, dark and dank canal alongside Weteringstraat. You're entering busier waters now, as you pass the Lido and its waterfront café terrace, then Leidseplein and the Art Nouveau **American Hotel ❸**, opposite which is another mooring where you can deposit the bike. Otherwise, to complete the circuit, pass the **Bellevue Theater** and the **De la Mar Theater** and turn right into Leidsegracht, which brings you back to Prinsengracht and a straight run back to Westermarkt. After returning your bikes go round the corner to eat at **Bistro Bij ons**, see ❶.

Tram outside Centraal Station.

AMSTERDAM BY TRAM

Riding Amsterdam's trams is fun, fast and convenient. This express–tram itinerary passes many of the city's highlights, and the new business and residential districts on the outskirts.

DISTANCE: 20km (12 miles)
TIME: 2 hours
START/END: Centraal Station
POINTS TO NOTE: You'll need an electronic OV-chipkaart (see page 120). Instead of taking the tram back, you could also do the return journey using Amsterdam's Metro, which is quicker.

Instead of regarding Amsterdam's trams as a means for getting from A to B, think of them as an inexpensive tour option. This route takes you past many major attractions and out into the suburbs that most visitors never see.

Start from **Centraal Station** ❶. Take the blue tram No. 12 from the stop to your left as you face the station.

MAGNA PLAZA

As the tram emerges from Centraal Station, keep an eye open for the 1629 brown café **De Café Karpershoek** to your right on the corner of Martelaarsgracht. The tram rolls along Nieuwezijds Voorburgwal

and stops at a building with pear-shaped towers that was formerly the main Post Office and is now the **Magna Plaza** ❷ shopping centre. To your left is the rear of the **Royal Palace**.

Note the excellent Indonesian restaurant **Kantjil en de Tijger** beside the tram stop at Spui. You swing around Koningsplein and into **Leidsestraat**, which is a notable shopping street. The tram stops on the bridges across **Keizersgracht** and **Prinsengracht**, giving passengers a fine view along the canals. **Leidseplein** ❸ is one of the places at which you might alight, for a stroll around one of Amsterdam's liveliest squares.

THE MUSEUM QUARTER

As the tram turns hard left onto Stadhouderskade, get ready for some rapid-fire switches of attention from right to left and back again. To your left is the **Holland Casino Amsterdam**, then to your right the entrance to **Vondelpark**. You veer into Hobbemastraat, with the illustrious **Pieter Cornelisz**

Tram stop outside Magna Plaza.

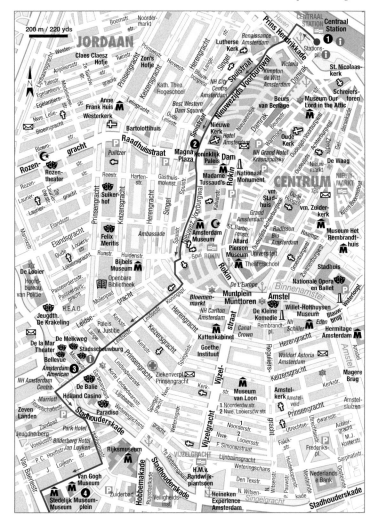

World Trade Center Amsterdam.

Hooftstraat shopping thoroughfare and **Coster Diamonds** to your right, and the **Rijksmuseum** to your left, then into Paulus Potterstraat, where, in quick succession out of the left-side window, you will notice the **Van Gogh Museum** and the modern-art **Stedelijk Museum**. Now the tram turns left into Van Baerlestraat, where the **Concertgebouw** lies to your right and the long vista of **Museumplein ❹** to your left.

INTO THE SUBURBS

Further on, at the Roelof Hartplein stop, change tram to No. 5, and travel on, turning right on a road leading to Beethovenstraat, from which point there are fewer landmarks to see and you can relax. Now the tram, liberated from the city centre's constricted streets, picks up the pace. The view is one of apartment blocks, at least until you reach the big, blue-glass-fronted **World Trade Center Amsterdam**, known locally as the Blauwe Engel (Blue Angel). Other modern office towers line the adjacent motorway until the tram turns left into Buitenveldertselaan.

The tram rushes ever faster through the dormitory suburbs of Buitenveldert and Amstelveen, until it takes a hard right off Beneluxbaan and stops a few seconds later at the terminus beside the **Stadshart Amstelveen Shopping Centre**. This is a good place for out-of-town shopping although, predictably, it lacks the character of the city centre.

RETURN JOURNEY

You might, for the sake of variety, decide to return on the express tram/metro line, in which case walk to Beneluxbaan. The imposing white building you pass on the way is another modern art centre – the **Cobra Museum** (Sandebergplein 1–3; www.cobra-museum.nl; Tue–Sun 11am–5pm). Take the express tram/metro line No. 51 at the Amstelveen Centrum stop in the direction of the Centraal Station. You will partly retrace the previous route as the metro uses a large portion of the No 5 tram line's rails. After passing the World Trade Center and the enormous **RAI Amsterdam Convention Centre** to your left and, by way of any number of tortuous twists and turns, and subterranean tunnels, beyond **Amstel Station**, the line runs underground, taking you quickly back to Centraal Station and perhaps a snack at **De Café Karpershoek**, see ❶.

Food and Drink

❶ DE CAFÉ KARPERSHOEK

Martelaarsgracht 2; tel: 020-624 7886; http://cafekarpershoek.nl; daily 9am–1am, Fri–Sat until 2am; €

If you want a traditional Dutch place close to Centraal Station, this café dates back to 1606 when it opened as a lodging house for sailors from the nearby docks. It's still a simple place, serving snacks and drinks, its walls covered with all kinds of ephemera.

Cycling alongside the River Amstel.

BY BICYCLE ALONG THE RIVER AMSTEL

Cycle along a fairly quiet riverside route and emerge in the countryside on the way to the pretty village of Ouderkerk aan de Amstel. There are no sites to visit, but you will probably want to stop at a café or a restaurant.

DISTANCE: 20km (12.4 miles)
TIME: 4–5 hours
START/END: Waterlooplein
POINTS TO NOTE: This is a good family option, to give children a break from city sightseeing, and because the Dutch cycle everywhere with their kids.

The bicycle is one of the most recognisable symbols of the Netherlands, along with tulips and windmills, but unlike those two it is the one that is closest to the day-to-day life of Amsterdammers. Everyone cycles everywhere, as it's the quickest and cheapest way to get around. More and more cities around the world are seeing the advantages of becoming 'bike-friendly', but Amsterdam grew up that way. You still have to take care, but at least most people – pedestrians, drivers and other cyclists – are aware that wherever you go and whichever way you turn, there are likely to be bikes around. This route offers a safe introduction to cycling in the city, and soon has you out into the country-side where you'll be seeing the advantages of pedal-power.

Start at Waterlooplein, which is served by tram line 14 and, stopping at the metro station, the metro and snel-tram lines 51, 53 and 54.

MAGERE BRUG

The best place from which to rent a bicycle in this district is **Mac Bike ❶** (Water-

Crossing the Magere Brug.

Royal Theater Carré.

looplein 199; www.macbike.nl), off the north side of Waterlooplein (see page 63). Once you have chosen a suitable model, cycle to the right (east) bank of the **River Amstel**, passing but not crossing the **Blauwbrug** (Blue Bridge) connecting Waterlooplein and Amstelstraat. Houseboats are moored along the river here and the scene on the water is likely to be quite busy. Continue to the **Magere Brug**, the 'Skinny Bridge' over the Amstel, an 18th-century replacement for the original 17th-century bridge. Note the fine local *eetcafé* **De Magere Brug ❷** (Amstel 81), whose guest book was signed by singer Rod Stewart, with the comment, 'Nice ham 'n' eggs'.

Cross to the left bank and continue south. You should be able to see the **Royal Theater Carré**, where Stewart had been performing, on the other side of the water. Continue over the tram lines on Sarphatistraat. You need to take a convoluted route now, diverting around a break in the riverside road, over busy Stadhouderskade and back to the river at **Amsteldijk**.

MARTIN LUTHER KING PARK

Keep pedalling south, enjoying the ambience, until you reach the **Berlage Brug**, where the traffic becomes busier. At **Martin Luther King Park ❸** most

Ouderkerk aan de Amstel.

of the traffic swings away on President Kennedylaan, leaving you still on the Amsteldijk, which is now almost rural, with houseboats in place of cottages. The thundering noise you begin to hear up ahead might sound like a Niagara-sized waterfall, but is actually the traffic on the A10 Ringweg Zuid bridge.

You're in the countryside now, passing Amstel Park and a pretty, if kitsch, scene of a windmill complete with a statue of Rembrandt. Beyond this is a great little café, **Het Kalfje**, whose riverside terrace is unfortunately on the other side of the road. (There used to be a road sign that read, 'Caution: Waiter Crossing').

The river is scenic and tranquil as you pass villas and cottages en route to **Ouderkerk aan de Amstel** ❹. This village has plenty of restaurants and cafés with waterside terraces, most of them owned by Holland's first family of cuisine: the Fagels. The village is good for exploring by bike. If you want to dine here, you can do no better than the **Brasserie Paardenburg**, see ❶.

RETURN RIDE

Switch to the right bank to return. This road, which becomes Ouderkerkerdijk, passes through some delightful hamlets and past another windmill. Recross the river at the **Utrechtse Brug**, which marks your return to the bustling urban scene. Take Amsteldijk to the Berlage Brug. At this point you can either re-cross and cycle to **Amstel Station** ❺, from where you and your bike can board a metro to Waterlooplein, or cycle back along whichever bank takes your fancy.

The Skinny Sisters

How did the Magere Brug get its name? *Mager* means 'skinny' in Dutch, and it would be simple to assume that its name refers to the narrowness of the bridge. Not so, say Amsterdammers, who will regale you with stories of two sisters called Mager who each had a house on opposite sides of the bridge and who paid for the original bridge to be built. By amazing coincidence, these two sisters were also thin, which prompts comments about the '*mager* Mager sisters'.

Food and Drink

❶ BRASSERIE PAARDENBURG
Amstelzijde 55; tel: 020-496 1210; www.brasseriepaardenburg.nl; Mon–Fri 11am–10pm, Sat–Sun 10am–10pm; €€
The chef in this cheerful brasserie specialises in market-fresh produce, with daily fish specials, but a choice of vegetarian and meat dishes too, including rib-eye and hamburger with truffle mayonnaise. The international wine list is short but with bottles at all price levels.

THE JORDAAN

The working-class district has been subject to gentrification, but plenty of its original charm remains. Allow two hours for this afternoon stroll.

DISTANCE: 2km (1.2 miles)
TIME: 2 hours
START: Noorderkerk
END: Westerkerk
POINTS TO NOTE: This is a relaxed stroll, best enjoyed on a sunny day to make the most of the Jordaan atmosphere and canal views.

The Jordaan is a very popular district for visitors, and a good place to be based. It has some lovely hotels in canal-side buildings, a range of great eating places, lovely views, historic buildings, quirky shops and an atmosphere all of its own. The area was built in the early 17th century to allow for the expansion of the city to the east, and it was seen as a place where the working people could live.

In the 1970s, parts of the Jordaan were earmarked for demolition, but thanks to widespread protests, the narrow streets were preserved, complete with period features such as ornate hanging street lamps. Despite the small size of many of the houses in this area, they are among the most expensive in the whole country. The Jordaan is *the* place to live in Amsterdam, and definitely a must-see for visitors.

Start this itinerary beside the **Noorderkerk ❶** at Noordermarkt. This is not on any of the city's tram or bus routes; to get there from Centraal Station, walk along Prins Hendrikkade to Haarlemmer Houttuinen and Prinsengracht. For a description of the Noordermarkt and Noorderkerk (North Church), see page 27.

THE JORDAAN

The great Golden-Age canals of 17th-century Amsterdam were intended to serve the homes of the landed nobility and wealthy merchants; the artisans and labourers were consigned to the Jordaan – a grid of streets and narrow canals cut east-west along the course of existing polders (drainage ditches). The Jordaan's name may derive from the French *jardin* (garden), possibly in ref-

A sunny morning on Bloemgracht.

erence to the market gardens maintained by the original inhabitants. Many of the streets are named after fragrant flowers, but this was not the prettiest or sweetest smelling area of Amsterdam in its heyday. Overcrowding was rife and with industries such as fabric-dyeing carried out on the ground floors, it was an unsanitary place to live.

BROUWERSGRACHT

Walk to **Brouwersgracht** (the Brewers' Canal), with its houseboats and rows of old warehouses now converted into chic apartments. If you want a coffee or beer, try the traditional brown café **'t Papeneiland** on the corner (see route 1). Otherwise turn left on Brouwersgracht, past a sculpture of the writer Theo Thijssen (1879–1943). Across the water the modern Blauwe Burgt apartment block exemplifies the way new and old are conjoined along the canals.

Go as far as Palmgracht, onto which you should turn left. Notice the sculpted tur-

nip on the gable at No. 28, a house dating from 1648. Then turn left into Palm Dwarsstraat and continue walking along Tweede Goudsbloemdwarsstraat as far as Lindengracht, which was once a canal. On Saturdays, a street market spreads its stalls along this road.

TRUE AMSTERDAMMERS

Off Lindengracht you will find **Karthuizerplantsoen ②**, a square that honours a now-vanished Carthusian

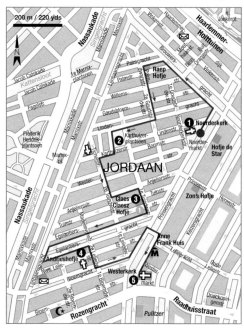

View over Jordaan from Westerkerk.

monastery. Adjacent Karthuizersstraat has a row of neck-gabled houses (Nos 11, 13, 15, 17 and 19), named after the four seasons: De Lente, De Zomer, De Herfst and De Winter. The **Huys-Zitten-Weduwe-Hofje** at Nos 61–191 has a tree-shaded courtyard with a double garden. The small houses here, now largely students' quarters, were once the homes of poor widows. Turn into Tichelstraat, from which you can see the Westerkerk tower in the distance: in much the same way that true London Cockneys must be born within the sound of Bow bells, so Jordaanese must be born within earshot of the Westerkerk bells. Cross Westerstraat, which was also formerly a canal.

CAFÉ STOP

You should now find yourself on Tweede Anjeliersdwarsstraat, and there are lots of cafés and small designer shops in this neighbourhood. Drop down a block to Eerste Tuindwarsstraat and Eerste Egelantiersdwarsstraat. On the way, between Tuinstraat and Egelantiersstraat, a passage on the right leads to the **Claes Claesz Hofje** ❸: two charming little courtyards surrounded by tiny flats.

Turn right on Egelantiersgracht, a quiet canal lined with some fascinating 17th- and 18th-century houses. On this corner, the hardware store at Nos 2–6 is an example of Amsterdam-School architecture dating from 1927. Beside it is another excellent old brown café, **'t Smalle**, see ❶, with a canalside terrace. There are three beautiful bell gables at Nos 61–5, one of which features a carved falcon. Don't miss the **Andrieshofje** ❹ at Nos 107–145, where a corridor lined with blue-and-white tiles leads into a flower-bedecked courtyard.

Retrace your steps, right into Tweede Leliedwarsstraat, and continue to Bloemgracht – one of the most impressive of Jordaan's canals. From here you can see the Westerkerk tower off to your left above the rooftops. The carved gablestones at Nos 81 and 77, dating back to 1642, represent a townsman, a countryman and a seaman.

To end your afternoon, walk back towards **Prinsengracht**, turn right, and cross the bridge over the canal to the **Westerkerk** ❺.

Food and Drink

❶ 'T SMALLE

Egelantiersgracht 12; tel: 020-623 9617; www.t-smalle.nl; Sun–Thu 10am–1am, Fri–Sat until 2am; €

With this brown café you have a choice of sitting in the cosy interior, or at one of the two terraces, one of them right by a canal. The food is simple and filling, and they have been voted Amsterdam's best wine bar.

The flea market at Waterlooplein.

THE JEWISH QUARTER

Most of the thriving community of the Jodenbuurt (Jewish Quarter) was wiped out in the Holocaust, but a number of Jewish elements remain in this distinctive part of the city.

> **DISTANCE:** 1km (0.6 miles)
> **TIME:** 1 hour, without museum visits
> **START/END:** Waterlooplein
> **POINTS TO NOTE:** Check the opening days for the Portuguese Synagogue, and buy a joint ticket to see both this and the Jewish Historical Museum.

There was always a sizeable Jewish community in Amsterdam, and they lived in different parts of the city. Many lived in the Plantage (see page 46) and others settled in the Jordaan (see page 60). It's on the edge of the Jordaan where you'll find the Anne Frank Huis. All this changed, of course, with the Nazi occupation of Amsterdam and the Holocaust. Ironically the Jewish community was built up in the city because many escaped from persecution in Spain and Portugal during the Spanish Inquisition. With them they brought the skills that helped establish Amsterdam's diamond industry. The systematic deportation of the Jewish population to concentration camps tore the community apart, and after the war only a handful returned to their homes. A visit to the surviving Jewish Quarter around the Waterlooplein area will reveal much about the Jewish contribution to Amsterdam's history.

Start at Waterlooplein, served by tram line 14 and by metro.

WATERLOOPLEIN

This itinerary begins with the multifarious offerings of the **flea market ❶** (http://waterlooplein.amsterdam; Mon–Sat 9.30am–6pm) on the west and north sides of **Waterlooplein**. In the 19th century the Dutch author Multatuli wrote of the market: 'There were headless nails, toothless saws, bladeless chisels, locks without springs, keys without locks, hooks without eyes and eyes without hooks, buckles without prongs…' You may well find that little has changed, except that there are many genuine bargains among the mess and the

The Muziektheater.

market is more business-orientated, with less ambience, than formerly.

'STOP THE STOPERA'

Just as construction of the metro line under your feet was the cause of rioting in the 1970s, so in the 1980s the nascent 'Stopera' building brought protesters and water cannon back onto the streets. The name was derived from the **Stadhuis** (Town Hall) and the new **Opera** ❷ that were built together on the square. 'Stop the Stopera' was the popular, but ultimately ineffectual, slogan; both institutions are now firmly established, and the Nationale Opera en Ballet building is a star in the city's cultural firmament.

JEWISH HISTORICAL MUSEUM

Cross the square and walk through the short Turfsteeg alley to the **Joods Historisch Museum** ❸ (Jewish Historical Museum; Nieuwe Amstelstraat 1; https://jck.nl; daily 11am–5pm) in the former Ashkenazi Synagogue, restored following its destruction in World War II. The museum has artefacts pertaining to the 400-year history and culture of Holland's Jewish community and explains the philosophies of Judaism, as well as examining the wider issues of Jewish identity. The displays feature paintings, books, and religious and household objects.

PORTUGUESE SYNAGOGUE

Cross over Mr Visserplein to the historic **Portuguese Synagogue** (Mr Visserplein 3; https://jck.nl; May–Aug Sun–Fri 10am–5pm, check online for rest of the year), dating from 1665. It was built by Sephardic Jews fleeing the latest bout of religious persecution in Spain and Portugal. Outside the synagogue, the Dockworker Monument honours Amsterdam workers – not just dockers – who went on strike

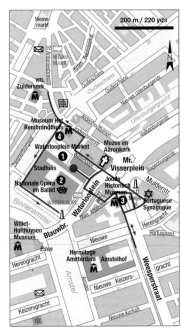

The Portuguese Synagogue.

Café de Sluyswacht.

in February 1941 to protest against the Nazis' deportation of the city's Jewish population. Unsurprisingly, the strike was savagely suppressed by the occupying Nazis.

Take Weesperstraat across the bridge over the Nieuwe Herengracht to the garden, which is on the right side of the road. Here you will find another statue relating to the Holocaust: a 1950 monument in the form of an altar, that is dedicated to the Dutch people who protected and hid Jews during the war. Retrace your steps and recross Mr Visserplein, past the neoclassical **Mozes en Aäronkerk** on the corner of Waterlooplein. This Roman Catholic church was built on a spot where, in the 16th century, Catholics worshipped in secret to avoid problems with the Calvinist authorities.

REMBRANDT HOUSE MUSEUM

Continue to Jodenbreestraat and Sint-Antoniesbreestraat, which was once the centre of Jewish life in the city. Today, the area has been partly redeveloped. You should visit the **Museum Het Rembrandthuis** ❹ (Rembrandt House Museum; Jodenbreestraat 4–6; www.rembrandthuis.nl; daily 10am–6pm), where the artist lived and worked until his bankruptcy in 1658. The house has been restored as closely as possible to how it looked at that time. Rembrandt's collection of rare and precious objects tells us much about Dutch society in the 17th century. Beautiful items from Dutch colonies in Africa sit beside Roman and Greek sculptures from the Classical era. There are a number of globes on display too, indicating the expansion of the known world in Rembrandt's time, together with seashells and strange stuffed beasts from far-off lands, and etchings by Raphael, Titian and Holbein. If you fancy a snack or a meal, nearby is the **Café de Sluyswacht**, see ❶, which is housed in a former lock-keeper's house.

Return to Waterlooplein and pass the Stadhuis. From here, continue to the black-marble **Jewish Resistance Fighters' Memorial**, which is located on the corner of the square.

Food and Drink

❶ CAFÉ DE SLUYSWACHT

Jodenbreestraat 1; tel: 020-625 7611; www.sluyswacht.nl; Mon–Thu 12.30pm–1am, Fri–Sat 12.30pm–3am, Sun 12.30–7pm; €
Dating from 1695, this one-time lock-keeper's house close to Rembrandt's House has two canalside terraces with great views. Inside is a traditional dark wood interior, where you can choose from their good beer list and range of simple bar snacks.

AMSTERDAMSE BOS

For a breath of fresh air outside the confines of the city, visit the large wooded park on the southern outskirts, where many Amsterdammers go to escape the stresses of city life. This is the countryside on the city's doorstep. Take a picnic.

DISTANCE: Up to you!
TIME: 4 hours
START/END: Centraal Station
POINTS TO NOTE: Try to do this family-friendly outing on a weekday, when the park will be more peaceful.

Fortunately there are many easy ways to get out of the city centre, which is quite a compact place – although 2.4 million people live in the larger metro area, three times the population of the city itself. While it might seem entirely natural, the Amsterdamse Bos, like so much of the Netherlands, is artificial. It was created in the 1930s, transforming what had been an expanse of open polders to the south of the city into a public park, not least to provide employment – this was the era of the Great Depression. All the work was completed by men and horses.

From Centraal Station take the No. 24 tram to **Amstelveenseweg ❶**.

AMSTERDAMSE BOS

If your stay in Amsterdam is long enough to accommodate a slightly out-of-town excursion, **Amsterdamse Bos** (Amsterdam Wood) makes for a nice day out. In the summer you can reach the park by old-style tram from Haarlemmermeerstation just north of the Olympic Stadium. This service is courtesy of the Electric Tramline Museum, whose collection of antique trams has been drawn from various European countries. Otherwise, from the bus stop on Stadionplein, take any

Rowers on the Roeibaan.

Cycling through leaves in the Amsterdamse Bos.

bus going out of town for several stops along Amstelveenseweg to the entrance to the Amsterdamse Bos. Or you could walk there under the viaduct of the A10 Ring Road and past the **Vrij Universiteit Hospital**, but you might want to save your time and shoe leather for the park.

The 800-ha (2,000-acre) park is an important ecological site. It serves as the home to numerous species of birds, insects and small animals. Moreover, it incorporates almost 160km (100 miles) of footpaths, and some 48km (30 miles) of bicycle paths. This means that even on the busiest summer day, there is plenty of scope to avoid the crowds.

The stables at Amsterdamse Bos offer woodland horse rides, a perfect way to clear the city air from your system (contact Amsterdamse Manege; www.deamsterdamsemanege.nl; tel: 020-643 1342).

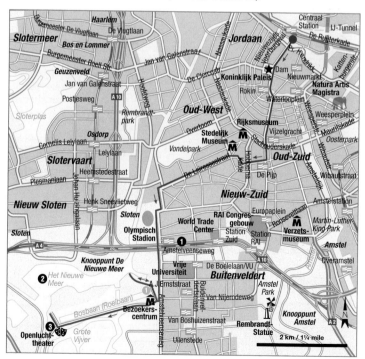

A path alongside the Roeibaan.

Take Koenenkade into the park. At the Bosbaan take a right over the canal bridge, then onto another bridge over a shallow inlet to the edge of **Nieuwe Meer ②**, a surprisingly tranquil lake on the edge of the busy ring road and Schiphol Airport.

THE ROWING COURSE

Follow the path to the **Roeibaan**, a 2.2km (1.4-mile) rowing course. At the eastern end of this long, straight stretch of water is a cluster of rowing stations and pavilions, where on most days you will see rowing enthusiasts setting up their craft. At this end of the rowing course is the **Grand-Café De Bosbaan**, see ①, which has a fine terrace overlooking the water. Alternatively, take a picnic and find a tranquil spot to enjoy these natural surroundings. Near the café, at the park's Bezoekerscentrum (Visitor Centre; open daily noon–5pm; www.amsterdamsebos.nl), you can trace the park's history and learn about the wildlife that can be found here. And just across the way is a stall where you can hire bicycles to tour the park.

Follow the Roeibaan to its western end (which is the start of the rowing course). Just beyond the first car park, lies the Dachaumonument, which commemorates those who were deported from to Nazi concentration camps during World War II.

En route you will probably pass a long line of anglers. Just beyond here is a self-service restaurant, **Boerderij Meerzicht**, which is probably the best of the park's eateries, especially for light fare such as pancakes.

OPEN-AIR THEATRE

From here, if you have enough time, you can choose to explore the great expanse of the Amsterdamse Bos proper, stretching southward to open moors where a herd of Scottish Highland cattle grazes. Alternatively, retrace your steps past the western end of the rowing course and take the tree-lined path to the big **Grote Vijver** pond and the nearby, 1,500-seat **Openluchttheater ③** (Open-air Theatre), where there are often performances on summer evenings, including touring productions of Shakespeare's plays.

You can hire boats and paddle around the pond or simply enjoy the scenery and fresh air. Don't forget you have to walk the length of the Roeibaan again to reach the exit and catch the bus back to the centre.

Food and Drink

① GRAND-CAFÉ DE BOSBAAN

Bosbaan 4; tel: 020-404 4869; www.debosbaan.nl; daily 9am–10pm; €–€€
Overlooking the rowing course in the Amsterdamse Bos, this café-restaurant offers everything from a simple coffee and a snack to a full lunch and dinner menu. There's afternoon tea, and a children's menu too, with a wide-ranging choice of international dishes.

Cafés on Leidseplein.

LEIDSEPLEIN

The Leidseplein area constitutes one of the centres of the city's nightlife, with many of its most popular bars, restaurants and nightclubs all in close proximity. It never really closes, so if you have the energy you can dance the night away and still be up to greet the dawn. This tour highlights some of the most interesting possibilities.

DISTANCE: 1km (0.6 miles)
TIME: 1 hour
START/END: Leidseplein
POINTS TO NOTE: This is a tour best done at night, to get the full feel of the Leidseplein, though you can still do it in the daytime and enjoy it.

Although the distance covered by this route isn't long, and there's some retracing of steps, it does provide a

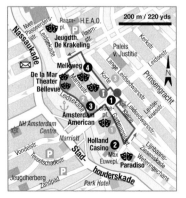

feel for life in and around the Leidseplein. There are more restaurants, bars, clubs, theatres and cinemas here than anywhere else in Amsterdam. The name comes from the fact that it was here that the road from Leiden entered the city, and although a 'plein' is a square, the Leidseplein is more of an L-shaped 'square', with lots of nooks and crannies to be explored. It was a popular hang-out for artists and writers in the 1920s and 1930s, but today it is definitely party central.

Start at Leidseplein, reached by trams 2, 11, 12, 13 and 17 from Centraal Station.

LEIDSEPLEIN

When planning a night out on **Leidseplein ❶**, it can be difficult knowing where to start. A clockwise circuit will help to familiarise you with its attractions. One of the foremost of these, at No. 15, is the **Bulldog Palace**. This gruff and bristly standard-bearer of the genre is one of the 'smoking coffee shops' for which Amsterdam is famous. 'Smoking'

The Stadsschouwburg (City Theatre).

refers to marijuana and hashish, both of which, though technically illegal, have been officially 'tolerated' in the Netherlands for years. Numerous foreign pot smokers make their way to Amsterdam specifically to puff their way through as much of these soft drugs as they can. In the Bulldog, as in most of these places, it'll mostly be tourists you'll be peering at through the fog of smoke.

THE CASINO

An extension of Leidseplein is a smaller square, **Kleine Gartmanplantsoen**, in which, at Nos 13–25, you will find the seven-screen **Pathé City** complex. These tend to show the latest releases from Hollywood with Dutch subtitles.

Across the street is one of the best café-restaurants in the square, **De Balie**, see ❶, a chic place that serves

great snacks on the ground floor and has a good restaurant upstairs. Left of the Balie as you face it is a passage leading to **Max Euweplein**, the home of **Holland Casino Amsterdam ❷**, the city's only legally recognised casino (to gain entry you must be properly dressed and show your passport).

THE AMERICAN HOTEL

If seeing and being seen is more your thing, return to Leidseplein. Across Leidsestraat is the Art Nouveau **Amsterdam American Hotel ❸**, whose stylish **Café Américain**, see ❷, is a showcase for Amsterdam's beautiful people.

Across Marnixstraat, back at Leidseplein, the **Stadsschouwburg** (City Theatre) at No. 26 stages most of its dramatic productions in Dutch, but it does sometimes feature visiting musicals from London's West End and New York's Broadway, as well as dance performances.

MELKWEG

For a less formal, more alternative experience, take Lijnbaansgracht next to the theatre to **Melkweg ❹** (Milky Way, No. 234). The heyday of this entertainment mecca was 30 years ago, at the height of the hippie era. But far from fading into acid-fuelled oblivion, the Melkweg has constantly reinvented its multimedia image – it has a restaurant, coffee shop, bar, art centre, dance

---

Going to the movies

All of Amsterdam's major cinemas screen international films in their original language (with Dutch subtitles). Given the ubiquity of Hollywood productions, English-speakers can therefore enjoy movies in their own (albeit Americanised) language. If you're more interested in foreign-language films than US blockbusters, don't forget that the film will be shown in, say, its original French or Italian, and the subtitles will be in Dutch.

Live music venue Paradiso. *A concert at Paradiso*

theatre, disco, cinema and concert hall among its facilities.

Adjacent to the Stadsschouwburg is a mass of busy cafés, the terraces of which extend into the square in sunny – and not-so-sunny – weather. Though they are all very much alike, the brown-café-style **Reynders** at No. 6 is particularly recommended (see route 2).

A short distance further along the street, at No. 10, **De Oesterbar**, see ❸, is a very popular seafood restaurant, while **Akbar** at Korte Leidsedwarsstraat 15 is a fairly reliable Indian option. On the other side of the square, on the continuation of Korte Leidsedwarsstraat, you will find **The Rookies**, at Nos 145–47, a popular smoking coffee shop comparable to The Bulldog but of a more mellow disposition.

MUSIC CLUBS

In a slightly wider zone around Leidseplein, embedded in a blur of cafés, restaurants and neon, are all manner of opportunities to sample live music. If you are a jazz aficionado, the music is generally of a high standard at the **Jazz Café Alto** (Korte Leidsedwarsstraat 115). You will find blues nightly at **Bourbon Street** (Leidsekruisstraat 6); and new styles of music at **Paradiso** (Weteringschans 6–8). If you're willing to take a tram for a couple of stops along Lijnbaansgracht, one of the city's best blues venues, **Maloe Melo**, is within range at No. 63 Lijnbaansgracht.

Food and Drink

❶ **DE BALIE**

Kleine Gartmanplantsoen 10; tel: 020-553 5130; www.debalie.nl; Mon 9am–11pm, Tue–Thu 9am–midnight, Fri 9am–2am, Sat 10am–2am, Sun 10am–11pm; €

The Balie was a 19th-century courthouse and is now an arts complex/meeting place. You can enjoy anything from a coffee while checking your emails to brunch, sandwiches and salads, burgers and lentil burgers, fish of the day, and several vegetarian options always available.

❷ **CAFÉ AMÉRICAIN**

American Hotel, Leidsekade 97; tel: 020-556 3010; www.cafeamericain.nl; daily Mon–Wed 6.30am–10.30pm, Thu–Fri 6.30am–11.30pm, Sat–Sun 7am–10pm; €€

The city's beautiful people like to see and be seen at the landmark that is the Café Américain, a stylish venue where drinkers and diners are surrounded by Art Deco and Art Nouveau. You can also sit on the terrace and watch Amsterdam go by.

❸ **DE OESTERBAR**

Leidseplein 10; tel: 020-623 2988; www. oesterbar.nl; daily 5.30–11pm; €€

This smart place is light and airy and with fish tanks lining some of the walls. As well as their oyster speciality there's fresh seafood galore plus a limited number of meat and vegetarian options. There are decadent desserts too.

Bars on Rembrandtplein

REMBRANDTPLEIN

Rembrandtplein has a more downmarket reputation than Leidseplein, yet it often seems even more intent on having fun, and you can certainly have fun on this route that explores the area.

DISTANCE: 2km (0.6 miles)
TIME: 1 hour
START: Muntplein
END: Leidsestraat
POINTS TO NOTE: If you have the stamina for a real full night out you can combine this with the Leidseplein route (see page 69).

Named Rembrandt Square in honour of the artist who lived nearby (see page 65), Rembrandtplein was originally the site of one of the gates into Amsterdam back in the 17th century. It was then named Botermarkt, for the Butter Market that was held there, but in 1876 a statue of Rembrandt was erected here and it was renamed Rembrandtplein. It's the oldest statue in Amsterdam. It's been a nightlife hub for over a century, a popular place for writers and musicians to hang out, and the numbers of cafés, bars and other entertainment venues just grew and grew till it became the noisy neon-lit place it is today.

Start at **Muntplein ①** on the corner of Reguliersbreestraat, which can be reached by No. 24 tram.

TUSCHINSKI CINEMA

Take particular care when crossing busy Muntplein to Reguliersbreestraat not to get hit by a tram – especially if you are accustomed to traffic being driven on the left. The grand multi-screen

Pathé Tuschinski

Escape, a nightclub on Rembrandtplein.

Pathé Tuschinski cinema (Reguliersbreestraat 26–28) is housed in an Art Deco masterpiece.

For a Malibu-style bar-restaurant-dance venue, go left on Halve Maansteeg to the Amstel and the **Bayside Beach Club** (Nos 4–6). Here the attempts to evoke the atmosphere promised in its name extends to the uniform of the waitresses – skimpy Stars-and-Stripes bikinis. If Dutch cabaret-theatre appeals, the **Kleine Komedie** (Amstel 58) is a great venue for what is a lively and inventively satirical scene in Holland, and housed in the oldest theatre in Amsterdam, from 1788. A few doors further along on Amstel is **Mulligan's Irish Music Bar**, where the music and the *craic* are so authentic you could be downing a pint of Guinness in Dublin.

If the Gaelic experience doesn't appeal, two local options might. At Amstelstraat 34 is **Gollem Craft Beers**, a pub with an incredible selection of beers. At the other end of the spectrum is the **Nationale Opera en Ballet**, the city's premier venue for ballet and opera, at Waterlooplein 22 (make your way to the end of Amstel and glance across the river).

REMBRANDTPLEIN CAFÉS

After seeing the Nationale Opera en Ballet building across the river, walk south along Amstel and turn right along Amstelstraat at the Blauwbrug Bridge. This leads you to **Rembrandtplein ❷**, a brash and brassy square that really comes into its own at night when it is awash with neon. At No. 46 there's a British-style pub, **The Old Bell**, see ❶, which, although somewhat ordinary, at least allows for a restful break and a snack. **Café Schiller**,

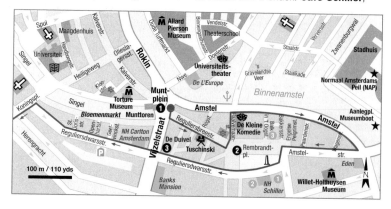

Royal Café de Kroon.

see ❷, is an island of chic. At the seriously smart **Royal Café de Kroon**, see ❸, drinking and dining is accompanied by cool piano music. For some local flavour there are other cafés in the square where locals and out-of-town Dutch like to assemble for a knees-up to schmaltzy Dutch songs.

Turn into Thorbeckeplein where, tucked in among numerous topless bars and 'exotic' floorshows, is a hot-wired jazz venue, the **Heeren van Aemstel** (No. 5). For Caribbean dancing and salsa parties on weekends there's **La Margarita** (Reguliersdwarsstraat 49), which is primarily a restaurant and café. Continue across Vijzelstraat to Leidsestraat at the end of Reguliersdwarsstraat to take in music venues such as **Duivel** (No. 87) ❸ and **Korte Golf** (No. 41) on the way.

Nighttime on Rembrandtplein.

Food and Drink

❶ THE OLD BELL

Rembrandtplein 46; tel: 020-620 4135; www.oldbell.nl; Sun–Thu 11am–1am, Fri–Sat 11am–3am; €

This English-style pub offers a cheap and cheerful dining option in the Rembrandtplein area, with an international list of draught and bottled beers, plus salads, snacks, sandwiches and other typical pub grub like fish and chips or steak pies.

❷ CAFÉ SCHILLER

Rembrandtplein 24; tel: 020-624 9846; http://cafeschiller.nl; Mon–Thu 4pm–1am, Fri 4pm–3am, Sat 2pm–3am, Sun 2pm–1am; €€

This historic Art Deco café has been around for over a hundred years, a favourite hang-out of Amsterdam's artists and writers. You can enjoy numerous wines by the glass and fine food such as perch with sauerkraut or steak tartare.

❸ CAFÉ DE KROON

Rembrandtplein 17; tel: 020-625 2011; www.dekroon.nl; Sun–Thu 4pm–1am, Fri 4pm–late, Sat 3pm–late; €€

The Café de Kroon is arguably the finest of the grand cafés, not least due to an excellent position overlooking Rembrandtplein. Both the cuisine and the decor are an amalgamation of Continental and Caribbean, and a palm-court orchestra plays at weekends.

Neon signs in the red-light district.

RED-LIGHT DISTRICT

This is a place many visitors want to see even if they don't want to participate. One of the best times to come is dusk, when the red lights glow with Japanese-lantern charm on the inky surface of the canals.

DISTANCE: 1km (0.6 miles)
TIME: 1 hour
START: Grand Hotel Krasnapolsky
END: Casa Rosso
POINTS TO NOTE: You can do this tour by day, when the streets are less-crowded – though the working girls will still be in their windows. By night, though, you get the full effect of the red lights and neon.

In most cities, unless you were a certain type of person, you would steer clear of any red-light districts. They tend to be in seedy areas that are probably not wise to be in, especially late at night. Amsterdam is different, however, as it is in so many ways. For one thing, the area is right in the heart of the city and it's easy to wander into the area by accident simply by turning a corner or crossing a bridge. It also has several popular tourist sites in or near it. If you want to see those during the daytime then see route 4, The Old Centre (see page 43). If you prefer to get the full impact at night, then let this route show you the way...

Start at the **Dam ❶** outside the Grand Hotel Krasnapolsky. There is no problem for women going around in groups of two or more but a single female might want to think twice.

'Cover me. I'm going in,' reads a folksy advert for condoms, a much-requested item of apparel in the red-light district. So, hitch your moneybelt a notch tighter and keep your hands where everybody can see them. We're going in.

Lots of visitors do this kind of itinerary out of curiosity or just for fun. You don't need to worry overmuch about crime as long as you stick to the busier streets. You can banter with the girls in the windows (most of them revel in their role as tourist attractions), but it is inadvisable to try and snap pictures of them unless you are dressed for swimming in the canal.

OUDE KERK

Take Damstraat at the side of the Krasnapolsky to the canalside on

Oudezijds Voorburgwal, turn left, and you're there. This is a fairly easy introductory step, as business behind the red-fringed windows doesn't start to get brisk until you reach the **Oude Kerk ❷** (Old Church, see page 44). Turn left into Oudekerksplein, and then left again into Sint-Annendwarsstraat. Stroll down the short Trompetersteeg from Sint-Annendwarsstraat back to Oudezijds Voorburgwal. You have literally to squeeze past the women in the doorways of this constricted alleyway,

giving them the ideal opportunity for a friendly form of marketing.

OUDEZIJDS VOORBURGWAL

Continue past the Oude Kerk and go right across the bridge. Turn right onto **Oudezijds Voorburgwal ❸**, which is really the heart of the surprisingly small red-light district. You might want to saunter into some of

The Sex Palace.

Sex and Drugs

Amsterdam has been cleaning up its act, clamping down on brothels and cannabis coffee shops and replacing them with higher-end cafés, restaurants, shops and galleries. Project 1012, launched by the city authorities in 2008, is aiming at reducing organised crime, drug-dealing and sex trafficking. But Amsterdam would not be Amsterdam without the bordellos and cannabis cafés so well over half the former and a third of the latter are being retained. Plans are afoot to banish all the bordellos around the incongruously located Oude Kerk (Old Church). Currently it is still overlooked by prostitutes bathed in the light of red lamps but also by the windows of new initiatives such as Red Light Radio, an online radio station where DJs broadcast from a former bordello.

Oudezijds Achterburgwal.

the street's many bookshops, video libraries or specialised appliances shops crammed around here. If you do you will encounter knowledgeable specialists in diverse areas of human relationships.

The Sex Palace (No. 84) is now the last peep show in Amsterdam, while Casa Rosso (No. 108) proudly considers itself the market leader in live shows. To bolster its cultural credentials it translates this description into several languages (in French, for example, the entertainment on offer sounds like a riverside village near Paris: *Baiser sur scène*). You will no doubt find a good deal to entertain, horrify, depress or bore you, depending on your slant, but Amsterdam's red-light district is definitely one of the city's more unusual attractions.

To eat in more salubrious surroundings, make your way back to the Oude Kerk where nearby **Restaurant Anna**, see ❶, offers upscale European dining.

Food and Drink

❶ RESTAURANT ANNA

Warmoesstraat 111; tel: 020-428 1111; www.restaurantanna.nl; Tue–Sat 5pm–late; €€

This smart place brings stylish European dishes at surprisingly affordable prices, though you can push the boat out and enjoy one of their tasting menus, maybe with a flight of different wines per course. Mackerel with mango and coconut is just one mouth-watering dish.

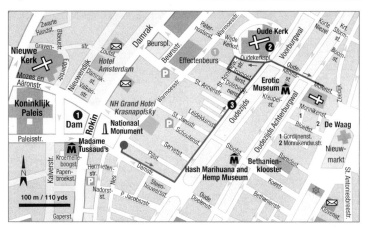

Haarlem Station.

HAARLEM AND ZANDVOORT

Haarlem can justifiably claim to share many of Amsterdam's advantages while mostly avoiding the hassles that go with the capital's famously tolerant and often eccentric lifestyle. Zandvoort is the destination for Amsterdammers taking a vacation at the seaside.

DISTANCE: 4km (2.5 miles)
TIME: 1 day, from Amsterdam
START/END: Haarlem Station
POINTS TO NOTE: You could spend 2–3 hours exploring Haarlem, with the side-visit to Zandvoort an optional add-on, depending on the weather and how your time is going. If it's a sunny day, you should pack swimming gear and suntan lotion for Zandvoort beach.

Although Amsterdam is the country's capital, and the largest city in North Holland, Haarlem is actually the capital of North Holland. With a population of only 160,000, it is a little like Amsterdam in miniature. It has the same fascinating history, charming atmosphere, 17th-century Golden-Age architecture, hidden courtyards – and plenty of canals too! Like The Hague (see route 18), it also has easy access to a seaside resort, offering visitors both a city break and a beach holiday as well. Choose either or choose both, but don't miss a side-trip to Haarlem from Amsterdam

Start from Amsterdam Centraal Station. There are several trains to Haarlem every hour. For Zandvoort, you usually have to change trains at Haarlem on both the outward and return journeys, apart from in the high season when there are direct trains too. The journey from Amsterdam to Haarlem takes only 15–20 minutes, and from Haarlem to Zandvoort another 10 minutes.

HAARLEM STATION

As soon as you arrive in **Haarlem**, take a good look around **Haarlem Station**. An Art Nouveau extravaganza dating from 1908, it can be considered as a destination in its own right. The moderately-priced **Station Restaurant**, situated in the former first-class waiting room, features pristine white tablecloths, conscientious service and, most importantly of all, wonderful cuisine. You might decide to stop here for lunch before going on to Zandvoort, or for dinner on the return journey.

When you emerge onto Stationsplein, walk down Kruisweg, which runs along-

Windmill De Adriaan, Haarlem.

side the bus station until you reach the Nieuwe Gracht. Cross over the canal and turn left along the waterside. At the Jansbrug turn right for a short way

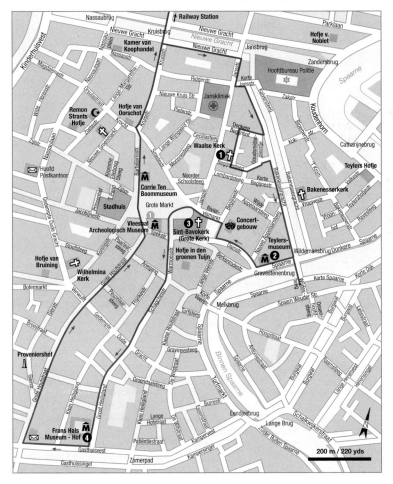

Teylers Museum.

on Jansstraat, then quickly left on Korte Jansstraat to the narrow canal called the Bakenessergracht, which is lined by pretty gabled houses, where you turn right at the water.

WAALSE KERK

The little alley called Kalverensteeg leads into Goudsmids Pleintje (Goldsmiths Square), where the goldsmiths' guild was once based, and then to the **Waalse Kerk ❶** (Walloon Church). This, Haarlem's oldest church, was built in the 16th century by persecuted emigres – Walloon Protestants and French Huguenots. The church is in the centre of Haarlem's old **Begijnhof**, whose tiny rooms, like their counterparts in Amsterdam, once housed religious women. Unlike that city's Begijnhof, however, they have now been put to a far less pious use: the Begijnhof constitutes Haarlem's **Rosse Buurt** (red-light district). Here you will find scantily clad women waiting behind their windows for customers from the streets.

THE RIVER SPAARNE

After circling the church, take Groene Buurt back to the Bakenessergracht and turn right. Look for the white, crowned church spire of the **Bakenesserkerk** behind the roofs on your left; maybe you'll hear its bells as you pass. Bakenessergracht ends at the **River Spaarne**, where, if you wait you're sure to see big canal boats passing under the Gravenstenenbrug. Cross over to the jetty from where the tour boats of **Woltheus Cruises** (tel: 072-515 9490) leave every hour for a cruise around the canals.

TEYLERS MUSEUM

Back on the other side of the bridge, you arrive at the distinguished, neo-classical facade of the **Teylers Museum ❷** (Spaarne 16; www.teylersmuseum.nl; Tue–Fri 10am–5pm, Sat–Sun 11am–5pm) which, dating back to 1778, is the oldest museum in the Netherlands. The Teylers exhibits an eclectic array of items but emphasises science, particularly from the 19th century – everything from fossils and minerals to brass-mounted scientific instruments. You will also find paintings, drawings, medals and coins, and the museum's elegant interior would be worth seeing even if there were no exhibits.

Next door to the Teylers is the **Waag** building (Weigh House), which dates back to 1597. It was built by the Flemish architect Lieven de Key, who designed many of Haarlem's most prominent buildings.

SINT-BAVOKERK

Take Damstraat to Oude Groenmarkt, where you will immediately see the imposing bulk of the **Sint-Bavok-**

A painting by Frans Hals.

Sint-Bavokerk.

erk ❸ (Saint Bavo's Church; www.
bavo.nl; Mon–Sat 10am–5pm, July–
Aug also Sun noon–5pm) in front of
you. Note the **Concertgebouw** (Concert Hall) on the corner of Klokhuis-
plein, then turn left into Rivier Vismarkt
where, at No. 13, In Den Uiver is an
old-style *proeflokaal* (tasting house).
Work on the colossal, high-towered
Sint-Bavokerk began in the mid-15th
century under the direction of the Belgian architect Evert Spoorwater. Han-
del, Liszt and the 10-year-old Mozart
all came to play the church's extraor-
dinary, 1738 **Müller organ**. Inside the
church is the tomb of the artist Frans
Hals (1580–1666), who lived, worked
and died in Haarlem.

Outside, the square is lined with
restaurants and cafes, many of them
spreading their open-air terraces out
onto the street at the first sign of
sunny weather.

FRANS HALS MUSEUM

Take Warmoesstraat at the side of the
restaurant, then Schagchelstraat and
Groot Heiligland. This is one of the most
charming residential neighbourhoods
of Haarlem. The **Frans Hals Museum
– Hof** (Groot Heiligland 62; www.fran-
shalsmuseum.nl; Tue–Sat 11am–5pm,
Sun noon–5pm), situated among a
cluster of old houses originally built for
Flemish retired gentlemen is one of the
city's foremost attractions. Hals is noted
for paintings such as *The Laughing Cav-*
alier and *The Gypsy Girl*, but he earned
his bread and butter painting portraits
of members of the local musketeers'
guild. Several of his pictures hang in the
museum, which has the world's largest
collection of his work, and which also
exhibits paintings by other Dutch masters, as well as collections of period
furniture, fine silverware and ceramics.
Look out for the beautiful 18th-century
doll's house. The second building of the
museum, the Frans Hals Museum –
Hal, is located at Grote Markt 16 (same
hours as Hof).

ARCHAEOLOGICAL MUSEUM

From the museum continue to the canal
at the end of Groot Heiligland. Turn
right, then second right on Grote Hout-
straat, following the street's continuation, Grote Straat – both of which are
major shopping streets – to the **Grote
Markt**. On your right is the 16th-cen-
tury **Vleeshal** (meat market), which
now houses the city's **Archaeological Museum** (www.archeologischmu-
seumhaarlem.nl; Wed–Sun 1–5pm;
free). On the Grote Markt is a sculpture of Laurens Coster, a 15th-cen-
tury local hero, by the Mechelen artist
Louis Royer. Haarlemmers will tell you
that it was Coster, not Gutenberg, who
invented the printing press. Work on
the **Stadhuis** (town hall), began in the
14th century; today the building features a tapestry of the Crusades dating
from 1629.

Zandvoort beach.

If you want refreshments, **Grand Café Brinkmann**, see ❶, is an ideal place for sitting on a terrace (in good weather) and watching the world go by. Leave the square by Bartel Jorisstraat and continue on Kruisstraat, past the 17th-century **Hofje van Oorschot**, to Kruisweg and back to Haarlem Station for the trip to the brassy North Sea resort of **Zandvoort**.

THE BEACH

From Zandvoort Station it takes only five minutes to walk to the beach which, in summer, is lined with *paviljoenen* (temporary beach cafe-restaurants). Topless bathing is almost *de rigueur* at Zandvoort – gays and naturists congregate at the south end of the long stretch of excellent sand.

Situated among the dunes just a stone's throw from the coast is **Circuit Park Zandvoort** (Burg van Alphenstraat 63) which, from 1952 to 1985, hosted the Dutch Formula One Grand Prix. Fans hope that what was once a highlight of the national sporting calendar will soon return; in the meantime the circuit still hosts less prestigious car and motorbike racing events.

AMSTERDAMSE WATERLEIDINGDUINEN

Aficionados of a quite different type of sport will doubtless appreciate the many charms – roulette, blackjack and so forth – of **Holland Casino Zandvoort** (Badhuisplein 7; daily noon–3am) behind the central area of the promenade. One of 10 legal casinos in the country, it applies a formal dress code (collar and tie for men) and a minimum age (18). And you will be expected to produce your passport if you want to gain entry. Away from the beach but still on the seafront you might choose to tour the **Amsterdamse Waterleidingduinen** – rolling dunes that constitute part of Amsterdam's legendary sea defences. You can roam on paths among the dunes on the seaside, and through woods on the inland side.

Zandvoort is not a particularly good place for shopping, but if you hit the centre of town you will find an array of eating, drinking and shopping options. A large number of the shops concentrate on summer clothes, beach accessories and all types of sporting goods that complement the resort's outdoor lifestyle.

Food and Drink

❶ **GRAND CAFÉ BRINKMANN**

Grote Markt 13; tel: 023-532 3111; www.grandcafebrinkmann.nl; Mon–Sat 8am–midnight, Sun 9am–midnight; €€
Haarlem has its grand cafés too, and none grander than the Brinkmann, which opened in 1879. It's now a listed building and having a drink or a meal here, inside or out on the terrace, is a real delight.

The causeway leading to Marken.

THE IJSSELMEER BY BIKE

This day-long cycling tour to Hoorn follows a narrow track between the polders and Lake IJsselmeer, returning to Amsterdam by train.

DISTANCE: 40km (25 miles) excluding return journey
TIME: 1 day
START/END: Centraal Station
POINTS TO NOTE: If you're a keen cyclist you might want to do the return journey by bike too, but if you're less keen or are travelling with children, the train back from Hoorn to Amsterdam is an easy option.

The IJsselmeer is a man-made lake, to the north of Amsterdam, and easily reached for a contrast to city sightseeing and a chance to 'go Dutch' and take a bike ride. You're sure to meet many Dutch cyclists but not so many other tourists. Until 1932 this area was the Zuiderzee, an inland sea, but then a dam was built which allowed the creation of Lake IJsselmeer and also the reclamation of lands. So much land was reclaimed that the Dutch had to create a new province in 1986: Flevoland.

Start on the ferry that leaves from the rear of Centraal Station. The dykes and

polders beside the IJsselmeer get very windy so wear appropriate clothing. This itinerary is a strenuous ride so various exit points are suggested.

THE IJSSELMEER LAKE

It's a good idea to rent your bike on the day before undertaking this itinerary to help make an early start. (Try Bike City, Bloemgracht 68–70, near the Anne Frank Huis; www.bikecity.nl) Cycle to Centraal Station and take the **Adelaarsweg-veer** (ferry) from the pier by the station, for the short trip to Amsterdam North (see route 6). Follow the road directly ahead, Meeuwenlaan, to a roundabout, and turn right onto Nieuwendammerdijk. Opposite a small lake the road veers right onto Schellingwouderdijk, which twists and turns beside the water before becoming Durgerdammerdijk. Follow the dyke road along the tranquil IJsselmeer shore, always keeping the lake on your immediate right. The IJsselmeer lake was once a sea, the Zuiderzee, until the 1930s, when a barrier was constructed to protect the low-lying coastline.

IJsselmeer dyke.

UITDAM

At **Durgerdam** ❶ the pace of life, which was never that fast, slackens further still. Typical of lakeside villages, Durgerdam huddles below the water level behind the protective dyke, with only its roofs peering over the top. Ride beside the houses or venture up to the dyke-top path, past **Uitdam**, with the sail-studded lake on your right and a grandstand view over the polders on your left.

Turn right at a T-junction onto the causeway leading to **Marken** ❷. (If you're short of time or stamina, turn left instead to skip Marken which, though beautiful, represents a major diversion.) Marken is no longer an island – the causeway connects it to the mainland – but it remains insular. The green-and-white-painted houses of the village are clustered around a tiny harbour to the left of the car park. The remainder of the island is given over to farming. A white lighthouse stands at its tip and *boters* and *skûtsjes* (old-style IJsselmeer sailing ships) ply the waters offshore. For a *koffie en appelgebak met slagroom* (coffee and apple pie with cream) go to **De Taanketel**, see ❶.

In the summer, you can take an excursion boat, the *Marken Express* (journey time: 25 minutes, frequent service), to Volendam, which means bypassing **Monnickendam** ❸ and saving yourself a fair amount of pedalling. Otherwise retrace your route back across the causeway, and stay on the lakeside road as far as Monnickendam. The harbour here has a vast array of pleasure craft, from little dinghies to gleaming ocean-going luxury cruisers, plus fishing boats.

VOLENDAM AND EDAM

Stick to the shore and pass through Katwoude on the way to **Volendam** ❹. The populist face of Dutch tourism is on display at Volendam. The locals wear traditional costumes – you can have your picture taken wearing clogs and short jackets, or long flowery aprons and milk-

Hoorn's central square.

maid hats. Harbourside fish-stalls do brisk business, especially with smoked IJsselmeer *paling* (eel). If by now you've had enough cycling, this is a good point from which to head back to Amsterdam. But if you still have energy to burn, go inland a short way from the lake dyke to **Edam** ❺, a charming town famed for its *Edammer* cheese. This is another potential exit point – you can keep going west of Edam to nearby **Purmerend**, which has a railway station on the Amsterdam-Hoorn line. If you're game for more, turn right at the canal bridge at **Damplein**, and right again to return to the IJsselmeer shore.

HOORN

Ahead of you is a long, straight run north through the polders beside the lake. The little villages of **Warder**, **Eteresheim** and **Scharwoude** are landmarks on the way

to **Hoorn** ❻, a living reminder of the traders and explorers from Zuiderzee towns in the past – South Africa's Cape Horn takes its name from Hoorn. The town wears its history on its sleeve – witness the care lavished on old sailors' houses, gabled merchants' villas, the Stadhuis (town hall) and churches.

It's worth visiting the beautiful inner harbour, the **Binnenhaven**, before taking a restorative drink at the **Hoofdtoren**, see ❷. Finally follow the green signs, pointing first to the VVV (local tourism) office, then to the station. Trains run every 30 minutes and take about 30 minutes.

Clogs

Clogs are traditionally made from freshly felled poplar or willow and after being shaped are left to dry and harden. They are traditionally worn two sizes larger than a person's shoe size, with thick socks to fit loosely to avoid rubbing the skin. Only ceremonial clogs (and those for tourists) are painted; everyday pairs are simple and unadorned. You often see farmers and sailors wearing them. Some road workers and deliverymen also find them more comfortable than standard protective boots.

Food and Drink

❶ DE TAANKETEL

Havenbuurt 1, Marken; tel: 029-960 2206; Apr–Oct Sun–Thu 9am–8pm, Fri–Sat until 9pm, Jan–Mar and Nov–Dec daily 10am–8pm; €
This cosy café/restaurant by the harbour, with an outdoor terrace for sunny days, serves soup, salads, pastries, and plenty of fish dishes. Also delicious desserts.

❷ HOOFDTOREN

Hoofd 2, Hoorn; tel: 022-921 5487; www. hoofdtoren.nl; daily noon–late; €€
This 1532 harbour tower is home to a bar, restaurant and a grill-bar. The grill offerings include spare ribs and pepper steak, while the regular menu adds lobster, catch of the day and a three-course set menu.

The Binnenhof.

THE HAGUE

This route takes you on a day trip by train to The Hague to see the centres of political power, and to stroll along the seafront at the chic resort of Scheveningen.

DISTANCE: 12km (7.5 miles), including tram and train rides
TIME: 1 day
START/END: The Hague Centraal Station
POINTS TO NOTE: There are two train stations in The Hague so make sure you get off at the Centraal Station. The route involves about 5km (3 miles) of walking, the rest being tram and train rides.

Amsterdam is a great city but, like any capital, it is far from representative of the country as a whole. This trip to The Hague, which has its own fascinating history, provide another view. It's one of the greenest cities in Europe and has a more relaxed feel than Amsterdam, though some Dutch call it snooty. It is also remarkably easy to get to its seaside suburb of Scheveningen, and enjoy the long sandy beach there.

From Amsterdam Centraal Station take the Inter City (IC) train to Den Haag Centraal Station (not to be confused with Den Haag HS Station). There are two trains every hour, and the journey takes 50–60 minutes.

DEN HAAG

The Hague is Holland's seat of government – Amsterdam is the commercial capital. In contrast with Amsterdam's laid-back, anything-goes approach, The Hague is elegant and refined. Commonly known as Den Haag (its official name is 's-Gravenhage), it seems less quintessentially Dutch than Amsterdam and, as befits the home of royalty, politicians and bureaucrats, it is well-heeled, and a trifle smug.

MAURITSHUIS

Emerging from Centraal Station into the broad Koningin Julianaplein, you can't help but notice, to your right, the monstrous **New Babylon** shopping mall and entertainment centre. Cross Koningin Julianaplein to the traffic lights beside the tram stop. Cross over to Herengracht and Korte Poten. To your left you should be able to see the top of the **De**

Girl with a Pearl Earring, Mauritshuis.

Resident twin towers complex, part of a gargantuan urban-renewal project under the aegis of several top international architects.

Keep straight on to **Plein**, an economically named square (*plein* means 'square'), with a statue of William I, Prince of Orange, presiding in the middle. At its northwest corner is Korte Vijverberg, on which, at No 8, stands the **Mauritshuis** art museum ❶ (www.mauritshuis.nl; Mon 1–6pm, Tue–Wed and Fri–Sun 10am–6pm, Thu until 8pm). In this palace, dating from 1644, is a superb collection of paintings by Rembrandt, Vermeer, Hals, Brueghel, Rubens and other important artists. A 20th-century highlight here is Andy Warhol's portrait of Queen Beatrix, while its major attraction is Vermeer's *Girl with a Pearl Earring*.

HOUSES OF PARLIAMENT

At the corner of Korte Vijverberg and Plein you will find the entrance to the

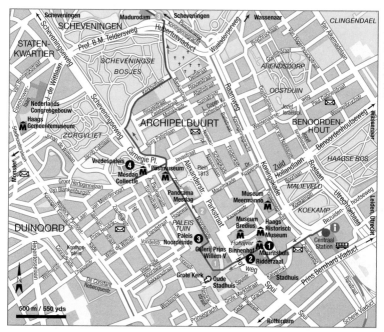

Binnenhof ❷ (Inner Court) of the Houses of Parliament (Mon–Sat usually 10am–4pm but check website first; www.prodemos.nl; tel: 070-757 0285). Here, in the 13th-century court of the Counts of Holland, is the magnificent, oak-roofed, gothic **Ridderzaal** (Hall of the Knights), where the sovereign officially opens Parliament every year. Both of the bicameral Parliament's debating chambers, and the Prime Minister's office, are located here. Pass under the western arch to the **Buitenhof**. To your right you will see the ornamental **Hof Vijver** lake, complete with an island, and fountain, in the middle.

Cross the road and walk to the far end of the Buitenhof. On the left side is the graceful **Passage** shopping arcade. Straight ahead you will see the Dagelijkse Groenmarkt, with the **'t Goude Hooft** cafe-restaurant, see ❶. A few steps past the restaurant brings you to Kerkplein and the 15th-century gothic **Grote Kerk** (Great Church).

NOORDEINDE PALACE

Leave Kerkplein by Grote Halstraat beside the 1565 Renaissance-style **Oude Stadhuis** (old town hall). Then take the pedestrian-only shopping streets, Oude Molstraat and Papestraat, to Noordeinde, where you turn left. On the road's left side is the neoclassical **Paleis Noordeinde** ❸ (Noordeinde Palace). This acts as the working palace for King Willem-Alexander and is not open to the public. At Noordeinde 123 is **Bistro Charrels**, a nice French bar/restaurant, see ❷.

At the end of Noordeinde, cross over the canal to Zeestraat and the **Panorama Mesdag** (Zeestraat 65; http://panorama-mesdag.nl; Mon–Sat 10am–5pm, Sun 11am–5pm). Painted in 1881, this is a restored, 120-metre (394ft) circular panoramic painting of Scheveningen, The Hague's seaside resort. You might recall the beautiful, fascinating panorama when you visit Scheveningen later in the day.

INTERNATIONAL COURT OF JUSTICE

Continue to the end of Zeestraat, and cross over to Carnegieplein, on which stands the **Vredespaleis** ❹ (Peace Palace; www.vredespaleis.nl; guided tours when the Palace is not in use: usually weekends and some days in summer, check website for times). Today the palace, built in the first decade of the 20th century with money donated by the Scottish-American philanthropist Andrew Carnegie, houses the International Court of Justice. If by now you have done enough walking, take tram No. 8 from Carnegieplein to Scheveningen.

There is one more place, a model city, which is worth walking to, but it is a fair distance away. Continue on Scheveningseweg, turn right on

The beach at Scheveningen.

Arny van der Spuyweg, then left on Dr Aletta Jacobsweg to arrive right opposite **Madurodam Miniature City** (Haringkade 175; www.madurodam.nl; late Mar–Aug 9am–8pm, Sept–Oct 9am–7pm, Nov–late Mar 11am–5pm). This enchanting 1:25-scale Dutch city features working lights, bells that ring, planes that taxi on the runway, and trains that run. Children and adults alike love it.

SCHEVENINGEN

To reach **Scheveningen**, take tram No. 1 or 9 from Madurodam and get off at Gevers Deynootplein beside the impressive, century-old **Kurhaus Hotel**. Take a walk along the seafront, and out onto the pier, where you are surrounded by the North Sea. The **Sea Life Scheveningen** (Strandweg 13; www.visitsealife.com/scheveningen; daily July–Aug 10am–8pm, Apr–June and Sept–Oct 10am–7pm, Nov–Mar 10am–6pm) is an aquarium with a glass tunnel surrounded by water, in which you can see sharks and other denizens of the deep in glorious proximity.

A little further along is **Beelden aan Zee** (Sculptures on the Seafront; Harteveltstraat 1; http://beeldenaanzee.nl; Tue–Sun 10am–5pm), an open-air modern-sculpture park. In summer you can relax over a coffee or beer at one of the many beach cafés or, alternatively, at the **Kurhaus**. For dinner go to the Tweede Binnenhaven, or Inner Harbour,

where you've a choice of restaurants including **Encore by Simonis**, see ③. Afterwards take tram No. 1 or 9 back to Centraal Station for the return train journey to Amsterdam.

Food and Drink

① 'T GOUDE HOOFT

Dagelijkse Groenmarkt 13, The Hague; tel: 070-744 8830; www.tgoudehooft.nl; daily 8.30am–midnight; €€
Located in a 16th-century building, with a lively outdoor terrace. The mussels are a speciality, though there's a wide choice of international dishes.

② BISTRO CHARRELS

Noordeinde 123, The Hague; tel: 07-281 0065; www.charrels.nl; Tue–Sun 5–10pm; €€
This relaxed French-style establishment serves up excellent steaks; the fish and seafood dishes are also well worth a try.

③ ENCORE BY SIMONIS

Dr. Lelykade 5, Scheveningen; tel: 070-306 0070; https://encore-bysimonis.nl; Mon–Thu 5–11pm, Fri–Sun noon–11pm; €€€
This classy place is one of the best round the harbour and they have an excellent Asian-influenced fish menu including lobster, salmon, tuna, crabs, prawns and sushi. Carnivores and vegetarians won't go hungry, either.

DIRECTORY

Hand-picked hotels and restaurants to suit all budgets and tastes, organised by area, plus select nightlife listings, an alphabetical listing of practical information, a language guide and an overview of the best books and films to give you a flavour of the city.

Accommodation	92
Restaurants	100
Nightlife	108
A–Z	110
Books and Film	122

Hotel de l'Europe reception.

ACCOMMODATION

For many years Amsterdam suffered from not having enough accommodation to meet the demands of ever-increasing numbers of visitors. That has started to change, although during the summer months and the popular spring tulip season, you'd still be advised to book well in advance.

That said, visitors do have a wide range of choices, from budget hostels through cosy canalside guesthouses to some of the world's best five-star luxury hotels, some with Michelin-starred restaurants. So where to begin?

Location is less important in Amsterdam than in many other European cities, as the centre is quite compact and most visitor attractions are easily reached on foot or by using public transport. If your main interest is in seeing the museums then it makes sense to stay in the Museum Quarter, not least because it makes it easier to get to them early and beat the queues.

The most romantic area is the Jordaan, so if your plans include strolling by the canals and having intimate meals in cosy candlelit restaurants, choose the Jordaan, which is easily reached on foot from Centraal Station, where the vast majority of visitors will arrive.

For older visitors, anyone with a disability, or anyone travelling with heavy luggage, there is one important factor. Some of the most characterful accommodation is in the tall and elegant houses that face onto the canals, where a room with a canal view is at a premium. Bear in mind, though, that some of these buildings are three or four floors high and, being old, many of them don't have lifts. Be prepared to lug your luggage, or make it clear you don't want a room at the top. Those winches under the eaves of some of the houses are still in use for hauling in heavy furniture during house moves – but they don't work with guests and their bags!

Price Categories
Price for a double room for one night including breakfast:
€€€€ = over 250 euros
€€€ = 140–250 euros
€€ = 90–140 euros
€ = under 90 euros

The Centre

NH Collection Barbizon Palace

59–72 Prins Hendrikkade; tel: 020-556 4564; www.nh-hotels.com;
€€€€

This large five-star hotel is next to the Sint-Nicolaaskerk and opposite Centraal Station, and it combines old

A luxurious suite at the Hotel de l'Europe.

canal houses with a modern entrance and reception area. There are several restaurants, including the highly regarded Vermeer (see page 101).

Best Western Dam Square Inn

12–16 Gravenstraat; tel: 020-623 3716; www.bestwesterndamsquareinn.com; €€€

Housed in the building of an old distillery, this cosy hotel has a thoroughly modern interior despite dating back to 1650. It's pleasant, quiet and friendly, and though it doesn't have its own restaurant there are dozens within an easy walk in this city centre location.

Estheréa

303–309 Singel; tel: 020-624 5146; www.estherea.nl; €€€

With its beautiful canalside location in a row of 17th-century buildings, the four-star Estheréa combines old Amsterdam charm and 21st-century facilities. There are crystal chandeliers and mahogany panelling, plus a cosy bar, and all the rooms are accessible by lift.

Hotel de l'Europe

2–14 Nieuwe Doelenstraat; tel: 020-531 1777; www.deleurope.com; €€€€

Justifiably regarded as one of the city's premier lodgings, this centrally located hotel is housed in a building dating from 1896, but beautifully renovated to offer five-star luxury accommodation. It stands on the banks of

the Amstel, where the river flows into the canals.

The Exchange

50 Damrak; tel: 020-523 0080; www.hoteltheexchange.com; €€€

The Exchange is one of the coolest spots to stay in the city. Creatively designed by graduates from the Amsterdam Fashion Institute, the 61 guest rooms range from one- to five-star: expect anything from Marie-Antoinette opulence to a room with a tent.

NH Collection Grand Hotel Krasnapolsky

9 Dam; tel: 020-554 9111; www.nh-hotels.com; €€€€

This imposing hotel stands opposite the Royal Palace on the Dam. The rooms are all shapes and sizes, in different parts of a rambling complex. The hotel has several restaurants and a pretty interior garden with an outdoor café terrace.

Mövenpick Hotel Amsterdam City Centre

11 Piet Heinkade; tel: 020-519 1200; www.moevenpick-hotels.com/amsterdam; €€€

What you see is clearly what you get at this huge, high-rise modern hotel, overlooking the IJ waterway just east of Centraal Station – the most stunning harbour views in Amsterdam,

Sofitel Legend The Grand Amsterdam.

and all the tried-and-tested virtues of a stellar branch of the Swiss chain.

Die Port van Cleve

176–180 Nieuwezijds Voorburgwal; tel: 020-714 2000; www.dieportvancleve. com; €€€

Just behind the Royal Palace, the hotel has an ornate facade and a historic Blaue Parade bar with Delft tile decoration as well as an excellent restaurant, Hulscher's. It's where the city's original Heineken Brewery was based, which moved when the canal out front was filled in.

Rho

5–23 Nes; tel: 020-620 7371; www. rhohotel.com; €€

This good-value hotel which has modern-style rooms is located on a quiet street but very centrally located, one block back from Rokin. In 1908 the building was a theatre and retains several original features from that time, like the Art Deco reception and lobby.

Hotel Amsterdam De Roode Leeuw

93–94 Damrak; tel: 020-555 0666; www. hotelamsterdam.nl; €€€€

This fine, medium-sized hotel, conveniently situated near Centraal Station, opened in 1911 but has been thoroughly modernised. The hotel's De Roode Leeuw, with its Art Deco features and wooden panelling, is one of the city's best restaurants for classic Dutch cuisine.

Sofitel Legend The Grand Amsterdam

197 Oudezijds Voorburgwal; tel: 020-555 3111; www.sofitel-legend-thegrand.com; €€€€

Built in 1578 as a Royal Inn, this building became Amsterdam City Hall following the loss of the Palace on the Dam and is situated in the heart of the old city. The exterior is an historic monument while the interior has been refurbished to an extremely high standard.

St Christopher's at the Winston

Warmoesstraat 129, 1012 JA Amsterdam; tel: 020-623 1380; www.winston.nl; €

Borderline-grungy, as befits an establishment bordering the red-light district, this hostel rambles through a large building with pretensions to an art-house style, attracting a mostly youthful clientele with bustle, a beer garden and an up-to-the-minute dance club.

The East

Arena

51 's-Gravesandestraat; tel: 020-850 2400; www.hotelarena.nl; €€

Close to the Tropenmuseum in Amsterdam-Oost, the rambling Arena is an eclectic mix of superbly restored monumental buildings providing the

The Grand's lavish interior.

A room at The Grand.

setting for lodging, dining, drinking and dancing that appeals to independent travellers. The contemporary-styled rooms range from studios to suites.

InterContinental Amstel Amsterdam

1 Professor Tulpplein; tel: 020-622 6060; www.amsterdam.intercontinental.com/en; €€€€

The 'grande dame' of Amsterdam hotels occupies a prime location on the east bank of the River Amstel. Exquisite interiors define a mid-size establishment favoured by international stars, top politicians, and leading business people. It also has La Rive, one of the city's finest restaurants.

Lloyd

34 Oostelijke Handelskade; tel: 020-561 3607; www.lloydhotel.com; €€€

An innovative hotel converted from a prison on the redeveloped harbour-side east of Centraal Station, the Lloyd has a well-deserved reputation as a cool place to stay, with artworks and cutting-edge fusion cuisine. Rooms are categorised from one- to five-star and priced accordingly.

Hotel Sint Nicolaas

1a Spuistraat; tel: 020-626 1384; www.hotelnicolaas.nl; €€€

This is a friendly, comfortable, modern three-star hotel that's conveniently located a few minutes' walk from Centraal Station. It has its own bar, and being modern there's a lift to all the floors. Rooms are for from 1 to 4 persons, and they're all modern but very differently designed.

Volkshotel

150 Wibautstraat; tel: 020-261 2100; www.volkshotel.nl; €€–€€€

With its basement cocktail bar and strikingly-designed rooms, this funky hotel based in what used to be a newspaper office appeals to those who like things a little different, and definitely quirky. There's a rooftop hot tub and sauna too, with city views.

The West

Ambassade

341 Herengracht; tel: 020-555 0222; www.ambassade-hotel.nl; €€€

Ten historic canal houses within a few minutes' walk of the city centre have been amalgamated to create the delightful Ambassade. The hotel scores highly for stylish rooms and attentive, friendly staff. It also has its own brasserie and a float and massage centre.

Andaz Amsterdam Prinsengracht

587 Prinsengracht; tel: 021-523 1234; https://amsterdamprinsengracht.andaz.hyatt.com/en; €€€€

Leading Dutch interior designer Marcel Wanders, renowned for his flam-

A suite at the Conservatorium.

boyant interiors, transformed what was a dreary public library into a chic hotel. The decor is playful and surreal, the atmosphere cool and the bedrooms luxurious. There's also a spa, a restaurant and a fitness centre.

Dutch Design Hotel Artemis Amsterdam

2 John M Keynesplein; tel: 020-714 1000; www.artemisamsterdam.com; €€
The large, modern hotel in the leafy but undistinguished western Slotervaart district lives up to its design-focused billing, and that, together with a waterfront setting and a De Stijl-influenced restaurant, might easily win you over. The lobby has changing displays from well-known and up-and-coming Dutch artists.

Dylan

Keizersgracht 384; tel: 020-530 2010; www.dylanamsterdam.com; €€€€
This hip hotel is housed in a 17th-century building with a lovely courtyard and terrace. Rooms all come in shades of white and oatmeal but they are furnished in four different styles. There's a Michelin-starred restaurant, Vinkeles, which serves modern French cuisine.

Hotel Hoksbergen

301 Singel; tel: 020-626 6043; www.hotelhoksbergen.com; €€
The Hoksbergen represents an uncommon combination of qualities:

high-standard accommodation in a 300-year-old house with a desirable, canalside location that is also good value for money. A characterful, comfortable option, and it also has five self-catering apartments to rent if you prefer.

Hotel Pulitzer Amsterdam

315–331 Prinsengracht; tel: 020-523 5235; www.pulitzeramsterdam.com; €€€€
The Pulitzer is made up of a terrace of 17th- and 18th-century canal houses converted into a warren-like hotel of charm and character. The furnishings are beautiful, the bedrooms – overlooking canals or gardens – sophisticated. There are several dining options, including the Jansz. and Pause restaurants.

Toren

164 Keizersgracht; tel: 020-622 6033; www.thetoren.nl; €€€€
Situated close to Westermarkt, the four-star Toren is a canal-house hotel within two neighbouring 17th-century buildings that together make up this boutique 40-room hotel. The velvet wallpaper and red, black and gold colour scheme gives the place a classic, warm look, while still being thoroughly modern.

The South

De Admiraal

563 Herengracht; tel: 020-626 2150;

Chic bathroom interior.

Old meets new at the Conservatorium.

www.admiraalamsterdam.nl; €-€€

This friendly, homely hotel is next to the tree-shaded Thorbeckeplein square in a building that dates from 1666 and is a Dutch National Heritage Monument. Room 9 has an access to a secret attic (now blocked) used by Jewish refugees and the Dutch resistance during the war.

Amsterdam American Hotel

97 Leidsekade; tel: 020-556 3000; www. amsterdamamericanhotel.com; €€€

Set amid the bars, restaurants and clubs of Leidseplein, the Art Deco American is a hotel favoured by celebrities and pop stars, and is a designated historic monument. The sound-proofing does a great job of cutting off the considerable noise that emanates after dark.

Apple Inn

93 Koninginneweg; tel: 020-662 7894; www.apple-inn.nl; €€

A place that looks as fresh as a just-picked fruit, this smallish hotel fills its elegant 19th-century town house just off Vondelpark with light, and features pastel-shaded decor, rooms that emphasise comfort and integrated design, and there's a garden at the rear.

Apollo Museumhotel Amsterdam City Centre

2 P.C. Hooftstraat; tel: 020-662 1402; www.apollohotels.nl; €€€

Just off Museumplein and Leidseplein, this good-value option for independent travellers has modern and comfortable – if not particularly distinguished – rooms, but scores highly for location. It has a cocktail lounge and a business centre, though no restaurant, but there are plenty within walking distance.

Bicycle Hotel

123 Van Ostadestraat; tel: 020-679 3452; www.bicyclehotel.com; €

The owners have turned their commitment to environmentally-friendly transport into a comfortable hotel for cyclists, which is pure Amsterdam. With solar panels on the roof and a recycling scheme, this is an eco-friendly place where, naturally, you can rent bicycles.

Conscious Hotel Museum Square

7 De Lairessestraat; tel: 020-820 3333; www.conscioushotels.com; €€€

Part of the Conscious Hotels chain, this small eco-design hotel opposite the Concertgebouw, has fresh bright rooms and contemporary hip decor. The breakfast is 100 percent organic, and there's an attractive garden. It's a good choice if you're planning to visit the Museumplein.

Conservatorium

27 Van Baerlestraat; tel: 020-570 0000;

Park Hotel tower room.

www.conservatoriumhotel.com;
€€€€

This see-and-be-seen-in five-star hotel was converted from the Sweelinck Music Conservatory in 2011. It is a stunning blend of old and new, transformed by Italian architect and designer Piero Lissoni in chic contemporary style, while losing none of its former beauty.

Dikker & Thijs Fenice

444 Prinsengracht; tel: 020-620 1212; www.dikkerandthijshotelamsterdam.com; €€€

Occupying a 20th-century house and a converted warehouse on the Prinsengracht, the hotel has lovely views from its canalside rooms. The classic-style guest rooms are a decent size and also good value for a four-star hotel.

Mozart

518–520 Prinsengracht; tel: 020-620 9546; www.hotelmozart.nl; €€

Close to Leidseplein, the Mozart is a modest but stalwart canal house hotel, squeezing decent modern furnishings and a few neat design touches into an old building's tight quarters, while regularly updating and striving to provide value for money.

Park Hotel

25 Stadhouderskade; tel: 020-710 7277; www.parkhotel.nl; €€€€

Across the street from Leidseplein and only minutes from Museumplein, the Park is a fashionable boutique hotel in contemporary style. Some of the rooms have fabulous city or canal views, and the trendy MOMO restaurant wins awards for its Pan-Asian cuisine.

Parkzicht

33 Roemer Visscherstraat; tel: 020-618 1954; www.parkzicht.nl; €

Reasonable rates and a fine location overlooking the Vondelpark are Parkzicht's greatest assets, and its budget rates attract a young clientele. The decor in the 1938 house is Old Dutch, while the welcome is friendly. Please note that not all 13 rooms have en suite facilities.

Pillows Anna van den Vondel

6 Anna van den Vondelstraat; tel: 020-683 3013; www.pillowshotels.com; €

On the north side of Vondelpark, a little way out of town, this unusual hotel, which was thoroughly revamped in 2017, attracts many like-minded guests. The thirty rooms and one suite are individually designed. There is also a bar/lounge and library and an attractive garden.

Prinsenhof

810 Prinsengracht; tel: 020-623 1772; www.prinsenhof.amsterdam; €€

Best Western Plus Grand Winston.

This hotel offers budget travellers a chance to experience life in an Amsterdam canal house, based in a central location. The beamed rooms are bright, clean and thoughtfully furnished, while the chance to enjoy breakfast with a view of the Prinsengracht is a definite plus.

Seven Bridges

31 Reguliersgracht; tel: 020-623 1329; www.sevenbridgeshotel.nl;
€€€

Sitting on one of the prettiest canals, this is among the most individual hotels in the city, with stylishly furnished rooms, stripped floorboards, oriental rugs and elegant antiques. There are no public dining areas, so breakfast is served in your room.

Waldorf Astoria Amsterdam

542–556 Herengracht; tel: 020-718 4600; www.waldorfastoria3.hilton.com;
€€€€

The iconic Waldorf Astoria is housed in six conjoined seventeenth-century canal houses. The rooms and suites have all been designed in neutral shades, and feature canal or garden views. There's a variety of dining options to choose from, including the two-Michelin-star Librije's Zusje restaurant.

North of the Centre

Amstel Botel

NDSM-Pier 3, 1033 RG Amsterdam; tel: 020-626 4247; www.botel.nl;
€

Noted for being the only floating hotel in the city, this converted river cruise boat, moored at the NDSM Wharf, a 15-minute free ferry trip from Centraal Station, offers compact modern cabin rooms at budget prices, some with harbour views.

Haarlem and Zandvoort

Amadeus Hotel

10 Grote Markt; tel: 023-532 4530; www.amadeus-hotel.com;
€

You won't get a better deal in Haarlem than at this simple, inexpensive hotel that is both cosy and comfortable, and right on the Grote Markt: ask for a room overlooking the square. All rooms have en suite facilities, and there's a good restaurant and lounge too.

The Hague

Best Western Plus Grand Winston

1 Generaal Vetterstraat; tel: 070-414 1500; https://plazahotels.de;
€€€

A few kilometres south of the city centre, the Grand Winston is worth the short journey as it offers four-star comfort at surprisingly reasonable prices. The rooms are cool and modern, and there's a stylish contemporary restaurant, The Grand Canteen, and a lounge bar.

Delicately presented seafood.

RESTAURANTS

They say you can eat in any language in Amsterdam, which is not far from the truth. The breadth of culinary options is matched by the quality, at all points on the price scale. The Dutch also like to get good value for money, which is reflected in the usually reasonable menu prices. Those prices, by the way, normally include the service charge so there is no need to tip twice unless you've had an exceptionally helpful waiter or waitress.

You shouldn't have any trouble finding a decent place to eat, anywhere in Amsterdam. The old city centre is so thickly populated with restaurants it's a wonder that the residents have anywhere left to live. Although the dense clusters of restaurants around Leidseplein and Rembrandtplein contribute to the colourful atmosphere of both those neighbourhoods, they do not necessarily represent the best of the city's culinary offerings.

Dutch specialities to look out for include Zeeland mussels, raw herring, smoked eel, asparagus, *erwtensoep* (pea-and-ham soup) and *hutspot* (beef-and-vegetable stew), as well as

Indonesian saté (grilled meat on skewers, with peanut sauce). Vegetarians in particular should sample the pancakes and *poffertjes* (mini-pancakes).

In general, any restaurant that serves meals cooked according to the Old Dutch style, even if it seems touristy, is a good bet. And, when the weather allows, dining alfresco on a restaurant terrace is recommended. If you are looking for a good, inexpensive meal try an *eetcafé*, the best of which are traditional brown cafés. By contrast, the grand cafés are sometimes rather pretentious. For something a little more ethnic, try an Indonesian restaurant. Many of the attractions, like the Rijksmuseum, also have excellent restaurants.

The Centre

Bird

Zeedijk 72–74; tel: 020-620 1442; www.thai-bird.nl; daily noon–11pm; €

This restaurant is always packed, drawing people for its authentic Thai fare. Bird serves up excellent meat and fish but vegetarians will not leave hungry either as there is a variety of vegetable starters and dishes to choose from.

Gartine

Taksteeg 7; tel: 020-320 4132; www.gartine.nl; Wed–Sat 10am–6pm; €

This simple place is run by a couple who grow their own veg and herbs, and have

> Prices for an average two-course meal for one, with a glass of house wine:
> €€€€ = over 100 euros
> €€€ = 60–100 euros
> €€ = 30–60 euros
> € = below 30 euros

Elegant Restaurant Vermeer.

Erwtensoep (pea and sausage soup).

an orchard too, so the ingredients are fresh as well as freshly-made. Try minced lamb with rosemary mayonnaise. Delicious.

Haesje Claes

Spuistraat 273; tel: 020-624 9998; www. haesjeclaes.nl; daily noon–midnight; €€

You don't get more homely than this old-fashioned restaurant, which fully merits the prized description *gezellig* (that cosy, welcoming, specifically Dutch quality). The steaks are particularly recommended, though there's an extensive list of fish dishes too.

Hemelse Modder

Oude Waal 11; tel: 020-624 3203; www. hemelsemodder.nl; daily from 6pm; €€

A mixture of vegetarian and meat dishes with French and Italian influences is served at this hip place along the canal from the Montelbaanstoren. There are also set-price three- and four-course options, and indulgent desserts such as frangipane and fig compote with lavender ice cream.

Kantjil en de Tijger

Spuistraat 291; tel: 020-620 0994; http:// kantjil.nl; Thu noon–10pm, Fri–Wed noon–9pm; €€

The menu and atmosphere are both cool and refined in this up-scale Indonesian place, where the food is a kind of Indonesian nouvelle cuisine. They have a choice of *rijsttafels* at different prices, including a vegetarian option.

Krua Thai

Staalstraat 22; tel: 020-622 9533; www. kruathai.nl; daily 5–10.30pm; €€

As well as Indonesian food, Amsterdammers love the spicy taste of Thai cuisine and the Krua Thai is one of the best in the city centre. The service is friendly and the fish dishes are especially good.

Nam Kee

Zeedijk 111–113; tel: 020-624 3470; www. namkee.nl; daily 11.30am–10.30pm; €

This abidingly popular Chinese restaurant off Nieuwmarkt could double as Amsterdam's Chinatown all by itself. It eschews pretty much anything in the way of decor in favour of authentic, no-frills Cantonese cuisine from an extensive menu.

Puccini Café

Staalstraat 21; tel: 020-620 8458; http:// puccini.nl; Mon–Fri 8.30am–6pm, Sat–Sun 9am–6pm; €

This is a great little café for breakfast, snack lunches or tea, with excellent salads, soup and cakes. The chocolate truffle cake is hard to resist as are the divine artisan chocolates in their sister shop, Puccini Bonbon, nearby at No. 17.

Restaurant Vermeer

NH Barbizon Palace Hotel, Prins Hendrikkade 59–72; tel: 020-556 4885; www. restaurantvermeer.nl; Mon–Sat 6.30–10pm; €€€€

One of the finest restaurants in Amsterdam, in a character-rich hotel facing Centraal Station. It serves an outstanding

Chocolates at Puccini Café.

French menu with Dutch and Continental influences in dishes like red mullet baked on ham or roast loin of roe deer with red-currants.

Sampurna

Singel 498; tel: 020-625 3264; www. sampurna.com; daily noon–late; €€

Sampurna has been serving classic Indonesian fare for over 25 years in this location. Satay skewers are excellent just as the main meat and fish dishes, or you can order a bunch of small dishes to share in the form of a rijsttafel.

De Silveren Spiegel

Kattengat 4–6; tel: 020-624 6589; www. desilverenspiegel.com; Mon–Sat 6–9pm; €€€€

There's been a restaurant located under this address since 1614. The today's restaurant, one of Amsterdam's finest and most expensive, serves up mouth-watering traditional Dutch food, with an incredible wine list comprising as many as 225 wines.

Vasso

Roozenboomsteeg 10–14; tel: 020-626 0158; www.vasso.nl; daily 5–11pm; €€

Authentic Italian fare is served in cosy ambience of 16th-century buildings. Polite and attentive service and a wide selection of tasty pasta, seafood and meat plus best wines from several regions of Italy.

D'Vijff Vlieghen

Spuistraat 294–302; tel: 020-530 4060; http://vijffvlieghen.nl; daily 6–10pm; €€

The historic and atmospheric D'Vijff Vlieghen ('The Five Flies') wends its way through five old gabled houses, and six dining rooms, each with a different slant on Old Dutch style. The menu includes eel mousse, risotto, lobster and beef BBQ amongst other delights.

Visrestaurant Lucius

Spuistraat 247; tel: 020-624 1831; http://lucius.nl; daily 5pm–midnight; €€–€€€.

Lucius, a block behind the flower market, specialises in seafood and fish dishes, ranging from huge plates of mussels to salmon and oysters. There is also a range of exotic species such as swordfish, and just sirloin steak for meat eaters.

The East

Café-Restaurant Dauphine

Prins Bernhardplein 175; tel: 020-462 1646; www.caferestaurantdauphine.nl; Mon–Fri 9am–1am, Sat–Sun 11am–1am; €€

This chic place is near the Prinsbernhard Park and serves international dishes ranging from mulligatawny soup and Iberian ham for starters to grilled swordfish, Lebanese salad and saltimbocca, and with a large seafood menu too.

Girassol

Weesperzijde 135; tel: 020-692 3471; www. restaurantgirassol.com; Mon–Tue 3–11pm, Wed–Sun noon–11pm, and sometimes the terrace opens for lunch in nice weather; €€

Portuguese cuisine is another style you'll find in Amsterdam and the Girassol

Exquisite chocolate dessert.

opened in 1983, the first Portuguese restaurant in the country. They put on *fado* nights occasionally in the winter, with a three-course menu.

De Kas
Kamerlingh Onneslaan 3; tel: 020-462 4562; www.restaurantdekas.nl; Mon–Fri 10am–6pm, Sat 1–6pm; €€
De Kas has some of the finest food in the city, served either in the spacious dining room or outdoors next to the herb gardens. The creative menu changes daily and focuses on organic ingredients.

De Magere Brug
Amstel 81; tel: 020-221 3400; www.demagerebrug.nl; Mon–Thu 11am–1am, Fri–Sat 10am–3am, Sun 10am–1am; €
De Magere Brug is an old-fashioned neighbourhood *eetcafé*-cum-bar whose customers include performers at the nearby Theater Carré. Dishes are simple, like burgers or apple pie, but there's a great view of the 'skinny bridge' from the terrace.

Wilde Zwijnen
Javaplein 23; tel: 020-463 3043; http://wildezwijnen.com; Mon–Thu 6pm–late, Fri–Sun noon–late; €€
This simply furnished relaxed restaurant specialises in modern Dutch cuisine, including the eponymous wild boar. Three- and four-course value for money menus are very popular here and really worth a try.

The West

De Belhamel
Brouwersgracht 60; tel: 020-622 1095; www.belhamel.nl; Sun–Thu noon–4pm, 5.30–10pm, Fri–Sat noon–4pm, 5.30–10.30pm; €€
De Belhamel looks like a *bruine kroegen* from the outside but the interior is much more elegant than the average brown café. Continental cuisine is served with a classical-music backdrop that creates a romantic atmosphere.

Bolhoed
Prinsengracht 64; tel: 020-626 1803; Sun–Fri noon–10pm, Sat 11am–10pm; €
With a great position beside the canal – and a tiny waterside terrace in summer – the 'Bowler Hat', housed in a former milliner's shop, adds a great location to a menu that brings zest to vegetarian and (for some dishes) vegan dining.

Duende
Lindengracht 62; tel: 020-420 6692; www.cafe-duende.nl; Sun–Fri 4pm–midnight, Sat noon–midnight; €€
Duende is a must if you like Spanish tapas, and if you happen to be in Amsterdam on the first Saturday or Sunday of each month, or the last Saturday, there's flamenco music too. They also have a tasty range of tapas and Spanish wines.

La Oliva
Egelantiersstraat 122–124; tel: 020-320 4316; www.laoliva.nl; Sun–Wed noon–10pm, Thu–Sat noon–11pm; €€

A table at Bord'Eau.

This Spanish wine bar in the heart of the Jordaan has a tempting array of early evening pintxos (Basque-style tapas) and an excellent choice of Spanish wines. Those with larger appetites can sit down to seafood starters or zarzuela (Catalan fish stew).

Pancake Bakery

Prinsengracht 191; tel: 020-625 1333; www. pancake.nl; daily 9am–9.30pm; €

This 17th-century canalside warehouse used to belong to the Dutch East India Company, but it's now been converted into a very popular pancake house. It does an enormous and typically Dutch range of outsize savoury and sweet pancakes, and children love it.

Pont 13

Haparandadam 50; tel: 020-770 2722; www. pont13.nl; Tue–Sun noon–late; €€

This floating restaurant in an old ferry boat is a little out of the way but worth it for the experience, though phone first as they host lots of private events. The short menu includes their own pontburgers, shrimp, rib-eye steak and lasagne.

De Prins

Prinsengracht 124; tel: 020-624 9382; www. deprins.nl; Sun–Thu 10am–1am, Fri–Sat 10am–2am; €

There's no friendlier place in Amsterdam than De Prins, which might explain why, at peak times, you'll probably have to wait for a free table. Moreover, the cuisine, which is both good and stylish, represents excellent value for money.

De Reiger

Nieuwe Leliestraat 34; tel: 020-624 7426; www.dereigeramsterdam.nl; Tue–Fri 5–11.30pm, Sat noon–4pm and 6–10.30pm, Sun 4–10.30pm; €€

This is a lovely old-style café-bar and restaurant filled with Amsterdammers, and with faded portraits on the walls. They offer excellent Dutch and European fare, including ribs and steaks. No reservations.

Riaz

Bilderdijkstraat 193; 020-683 6453; www.riaz. nl; Mon–Fri 1–9pm, Sun 2–9pm; €

Amsterdam has lots of good Surinamese restaurants, and Riaz is rated highly. If you're not sure about the menu, just ask and the owner will explain. Try one of their roti dishes, or nasi goreng, and they also serve Indian-style curries.

Toscanini

Lindengracht 75; tel: 0517-395 356; www. toscanini.nl; Mon–Tue 4.30–8pm, Wed–Sun 4.30–9pm; €€

This place in the Jordaan is always busy, which lets you know how good its pizzas are. The open kitchen adds to the lively buzz, and there are plenty of meat, fish and pasta dishes available too.

Van Puffelen

Prinsengracht 375–377; tel: 020-624 6270; www.restaurantvanpuffelen.com; Mon–Thu

Hotel de l'Europe exterior.

Michelin-starred cuisine at Bord'Eau.

4pm–late, Fri 1pm–late, Sat–Sun noon–late; €–€€

The Puffelen is a canalside building that on one side is the perfect brown café and on the other is an excellent restaurant that is casual but serves gourmet-quality food. There's also a barge moored on the canal that's open in the summer.

Yam Yam

Frederick Hendrikstraat 88–90; tel: 020-681 5097; www.yamyam.nl; Tue–Sun 5.30pm–late; €

This trattoria is a favourite haunt of locals for its reasonably-priced stone-oven pizzas and fresh pasta. Tables spill out on to a terrace in the summer, and it's nearly always full so reserve a table or be prepared to queue.

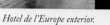

The South

De Blauwe Hollander

Leidsekruisstraat 28; tel: 020-623 3014; www.deblauwehollander.nl; daily noon–11pm; €€

A cheap and cheerful eatery, where diners eat in sociable proximity at large tables in a cosy setting. The dishes – stews, soups, steaks – are straightforward and wholesome, if not particularly exciting.

Bord'Eau

Hôtel de l'Europe, Nieuwe Doelenstraat 2; tel: 020-531 1777; www.deleurope.com; Tue–Fri noon–2.30pm and 6.30–10.30pm, Sat 6.30–10.30pm; €€€

Another restaurant situated in a hotel, the Bord'Eau offers a smart, fashionable gastronomic experience which has gained it two Michelin stars. The menu is Dutch and Continental, and there are five- and six-course tasting menus on offer till 9.30pm.

Dynasty

Reguliersdwarsstraat 30; tel: 020-626 8400; www.restaurantdynasty.nl; Wed–Mon 5.30–10.30pm; €€

This place close to Koningsplein offers a tempting choice of Thai, Vietnamese and Chinese dishes all conveniently under one roof. You can choose from the set menus or go à la carte to mix and match your meal from different countries.

Le Garage

Ruysdaelstraat 54–6; tel: 020-679 7176; http://restaurantlegarage.nl; Mon–Sat 6–11pm; €€

This exciting bar/brasserie near the Rijksmuseum is owned by TV chef Joop Braakhekke. The atmosphere is bright and breezy and the food is French influenced, with a fixed-price three-course menu available as well as à la carte.

Golden Temple

Utrechtsestraat 126; tel: 020-626 8560; www.restaurantgoldentemple.com; daily 5–9.30pm; €

Some people come to the Golden Temple vegetarian restaurant for the excellent salad buffet it provides, while others prefer the main courses featuring an incredibly creative mix of Indian, Middle Eastern, Japanese and Mexican dishes.

Riverside views at La Rive.

Izakaya

Albert Cuypstraat 2–6; tel: 020-305 3090; www.izakaya-amsterdam.com; Mon–Wed noon–2.30pm and 6–11pm, Thu noon–2.30pm and 6–11.30pm, Fri noon–2.30pm and 6–11.30pm, Sat noon–3pm and 6–11.30pm, Sun noon–4pm and 6–11pm; €€€

Come with well-lined pockets for this Japanese culinary experience in the chic Sir Albert Hotel. The dishes are made to be shared: think oysters in filo pastry with wasabi sauce and caviar, dim sum of scallops with truffle sauce and succulent beef from beer-drinking Japanese cows.

Loetje

Johannes Vermeerstraat 52; tel: 020-662 8173; www.loetje.nl; daily 10am–10.30pm; €€

This *eetcafé* claims to have the best steaks in Amsterdam, and its conservatory is certainly a lovely location in which to put that to the test. There's a terrace too, and the place is always busy, which tells you something.

Mamouche

Quellijnstraat 104; tel: 020-670 0736; www. restaurantmamouche.nl; Tue–Sun 5–11pm; €€

Amsterdam's Pijp district, south of the city centre, is a multi-ethnic neighbourhood and this chic place shows Moroccan food at its best with wonderful couscous and tagines. There are also some Moroccan wines on the international wine list.

Pheun Thai

Hobbemakade 71; tel: 020-427 4537; www. pheun-thai.nl; daily 5–10pm; €

As usual, if you want a good, cheap meal in a pricier part of the city, look to the ethnic restaurants. This is more like a café, but the food is fabulous. Try the wonderful chicken and shrimp with mango.

La Rive

InterContinental Amstel Hotel, Professor Tulpplein 1; tel: 020-520 3264; www. restaurantlarive.nl; daily 6.30–10pm; €€€€

This intimate and elegant riverside hotel restaurant specialises in elaborate French cuisine. The service, which is on the formal side, is flawless. You can dine at the chef's table in the middle of the kitchen of this Michelin-starred restaurant.

Roses by SAL

Reguliersdwarsstraat 40; tel: 020-625 9797; www.roses-amsterdam.nl; daily 5.30pm– late; €€

This busy place is behind the flower market and serves large portions of Tex-Mex cuisine, including enchiladas, tortillas, fajitas and sizzling chimichangas, plus a range of burgers. Pitchers of margarita are also available.

Sama Sebo

Pieter Cornelisz Hooftstraat 27, tel: 020-662 8146; www.samasebo.nl; Mon–Sat 9am–1am; €

Sama Sebo serves classic Indonesian fare, the authenticity of which is complemented by a profusion of mats made from

Haute cuisine at La Rive.

rushes and batik. Try their *rijsttafel* ('rice table'), a selection of 20 or 30 little dishes that represent a cross-section of Indonesian cuisine.

Warung Spang Makandra

Gerard Doustraat 39; tel: 020-670 5081; www.spangmakandra.nl; Mon–Sat 11am–10pm, Sun 1–10pm; €

This friendly and cosy place opened in 1978 and has been serving its mix of Indonesian and Surinamese dishes ever since. Whether you go for the soups, the gado gado, the rendang or anything else, you really can't go wrong here.

MarrakeZ

Gedempte Oude Gracht 11, Haarlem; tel: 023-844 5635; www.marrakez.nl; Tue 9am–4pm, Wed–Sat 9am–11pm; €€

This restaurant serves up tasty Moroccan fare. Arabic high teas with homemade scones and sweet bites can also be enjoyed from 1 to 3.30pm.

Restaurant Mr and Mrs

Lange Veerstraat 4, Haarlem; tel: 023 531 5935; http://restaurantmrandmrs.nl; Tue–Sat 5–10pm; €€–€€€

This unusual restaurant offers truly creative dishes, with the option of warm or cold starters and a dessert, or trying one of the chef's surprise four-, five- or six-course tasting menus. Either way it's an absolute winner for gourmet cuisine at reasonable prices.

The Wolfhound Irish Bar and Kitchen

Riviervismarkt 9, Haarlem; tel: 023 525 9054; www.thewolfhound.nl; Mon–Tue 4pm–midnight, Wed 3pm–midnight, Thu 3pm–3am, Fri–Sat noon–3am, Sun noon–midnight; €

If you want straightforward pub grub and a lively bar, then head for The Wolfhound which serves soups, salads, burgers and typical dishes like fish and chips. There's also live music most weekend nights, but check first.

Restaurant Basaal

Dunne Bierkade 3, The Hague; tel: 070-427 6888; http://restaurantbasaal.nl; Tue–Sat 6pm–late; €€

Awarded a BIB Gourmand by the Michelin Guide, this classy place serves a combination of Dutch and Belgian cuisine and has a special fixed-price BIB Gourmand three-course menu as well as four-, five- and six-course tasting menus.

Calla's

Laan van Roos en Doorn 51a, The Hague; tel: 070-345 5866; http://restaurantcallas.nl; Tue–Fri noon–2pm and 6.30–10pm, Sat 6.30–10pm; €€€

If you decide to stay overnight in The Hague, consider treating yourself to a meal at this ultra-stylish Michelin-starred restaurant where Dutch chef Marcel van der Kleijn offers elaborate multi-flavoured dishes, with five-, six- and seven-course tasting menus also available.

The Concertgebouw.

NIGHTLIFE

Amsterdam is well-known for its vibrant nightlife – a scene that runs the gamut from the high culture of sophisticated venues for classical music, opera, theatre and dance, to the notoriously erotic and sometimes sleazy dens of the red-light district. In between are the numerous, frequently bohemian, haunts of contemporary café society, plus lots of cabaret venues, nightclubs and the latest in music clubs, making it one of the clubbing capitals of Europe. Rock music fans will find plenty of venues, large and small, and the same multi-national outlook that fuels the city's culinary scene works on its music too. There are world music venues, as well as clubs specialising in jazz, blues, reggae and other music styles.

Music, theatre and dance

The local theatre scene is excellent, but you're unlikely to appreciate it unless you understand Dutch, the language spoken in virtually all local productions. If you are a real theatre aficionado, however, it's worth checking the listings and programmes during your visit, as there may well be one or two performances in English. You're more likely to find some English performances in the lively local cabaret and comedy scene, with some intimate clubs in the popular nightlife areas such as Leidseplein, Rembrandtplein and Waterlooplein.

Beurs van Berlage

243 Damrak; tel: 020-530 4141; www.beursvanberlage.nl
The Beurs van Berlage, the beautiful old Stock Exchange building near the Dam dates from 1903. Transformed into a concert and conference venue, for many years it used to be the home of both the Netherlands Philharmonic Orchestra and the Netherlands Chamber Orchestra.

Concertgebouw

2–6 Concertgebouwplein; tel: 0900 671 8345 (within Netherlands), 020-671 8345 (from outside Netherlands); www.concertgebouw.nl
The prosaically named Concertgebouw ('Concert Building') is one of the world's most illustrious concert halls with superb acoustics. The city's leading venue for classical music, it's home to the renowned Concertgebouw Orchestra.

Nationale Opera & Ballet

Amstel 3; tel: 020-625 5455; www.operaballet.nl
The Nationale Opera & Ballet building is an excellent setting for ballet and opera. The construction of the building was controversial but it has become one of the city's most popular cultural venues.

Royal Theatre Carré

115–125 Amstel; tel: 0900 252 5255 (within Netherlands), 020-524 9453 (from outside Netherlands); https://carre.nl

Paradiso.

This big theatre on the banks of the Amstel was built in 1887 as the home of the Circus Carré but it now features well-known international music acts. Musicals may be in Dutch or in English, with many of the latter performed by touring companies from London and New York.

Stadsschouwburg

26 Leidseplein; tel: 020-624 2311; http://stadsschouwburgamsterdam.nl

Despite the name meaning the Municipal Theatre, the opera and dance productions staged here tend to be more avant-garde than the shows at the Nationale Opera & Ballet building. It's worth seeing for the building alone, which dates back to 1894.

Nightlife

Johan Cruyff ArenA

ArenA Boulevard 1 (Amsterdam Zuidoost); tel: 020-311 1333; www.johancruijffarena.nl

The ArenA is the impressive stadium of the Ajax Amsterdam football team, and it also becomes a venue for big-name concerts from time to time. Tina Turner was the first to play there and names like Madonna, The Rolling Stones and U2 have all performed there too.

Bluescafé Maloe Melo

163 Lijnbaansgracht; tel: 020-420 4592; www.maloemelo.com; Sun–Thu 9pm–3am, Fri–Sat 9pm–4am

The Maloe Melo opened in 1998 and still features live music every night of the week in a suitably laid-back atmosphere. Though it's a blues club, the acts include rock, reggae, soul, country, rockabilly and world music.

Bourbon Street

6 Leidsekruisstraat; tel: 020-623 3440; www.bourbonstreet.nl; Sun–Thu 10pm–4am, Fri–Sat 10am–5pm; free on Mon–Sun, before 11pm Wed–Thu

Bourbon Street is one of the best jazz venues in town for mainly mainstream jazz, but some of the musicians – international as well as Dutch - veer into blues, rock and other genres.

Melkweg

234 Lijnbaansgracht; tel: 020-531 8181; www.melkweg.nl

Located in a former dairy factory, the Melkweg (Milky Way) is a long-established venue which is something of a relic from the flower-power, marijuana-fuelled days of the 1960s. Now the hippie aesthetic has given way to multimedia chic, and the Melkweg features a dance floor, a theatre, a lecture hall and a cinema as well as music.

Paradiso

6–8 Weteringschans; tel: 020-626 4521; www.paradiso.nl

Housed in a former church, the Paradiso is now a multi-media arts centre that grew out of the 1960s counter-culture movement. It features both big names and unknown acts, and people as varied as The Rolling Stones, Prince, Amy Winehouse, Lucinda Williams, Pink Floyd and Frank Zappa have all played here.

Navigating your way around the city is fairly easy.

A–Z

A

Age restrictions

The age of consent in the Netherlands is 16. The age-limit for driving recently dropped from 18 to 17 years old while the age limit for buying alcoholic beverages was raised in 2014 from 16 to 18 years old.

B

Budgeting

Average costs in euros:

Glass of beer or house wine: €3–5
Main course at a restaurant: budget €8–10; moderate €15–20; expensive €30–40
Room for two including breakfast: cheap hotel €60; moderate hotel €120; deluxe hotel €200
Taxi to/from Schipol Airport: €30–50
Single bus/metro ticket: €3 (valid for one hour)
One-day travelcard: €7.50
Tourist cards: You can buy an I amsterdam card City Card (www.iamsterdam.com) from I amsterdam visitor centres and many other outlets which provides free use of public transport and admission to numerous attractions, including over 60 museums (but not the Anne Frank Huis). Cards are valid for one day (€59), two

days (€74), three days (€87) and four days (€98).

C

Children

Amsterdam is a very child-friendly city, and right in the city centre you'll see parents cycling with their children, or sometimes carrying young children on child seats or pulling them in carts behind them. Reduced-price admissions are available everywhere, and reduced prices on public transport. Many hotels can arrange baby-sitting services. Some use the Babysitters Club, which you can also use yourself through their Dutch/English website: www.babysittersclub.nl.

Climate

Amsterdam's average winter daytime temperatures are around 5°C (41°F), falling to 1°C (34°F) at night, although temperatures can plummet to −10°C (14°F). The summer average is 22°C (72°F), falling to around 13°C (55°F) at night. Rain occurs year-round, but spring is generally the driest time.

Clothing

Even in summer it's a good idea to bring a sweater or cardigan because the evenings can be cool. Moreover, due to Amsterdam's proximity to the sea, the weather can change quickly. An umbrella

is a vital accessory at almost any time. Warm clothes are essential in winter.

Crime and safety

Amsterdam is not particularly violent, but, as is the case in most major Western cities, petty crime is a problem. Exercise caution in the red-light district and beware of thieves and pickpockets, especially in crowded areas. Some scam artists and beggars prey on people emerging from Centraal Station, especially if they look new to the city. Be vigilant, especially if someone tries to distract you, which usually means someone else is nearby waiting an opportunity to snatch something. The same applies on trains travelling into Centraal Station: keep an eye on your luggage at all times and be suspicious if someone tries to distract your attention: telling you that you have something spilled on your clothing is a common decoy tactic.

Customs

EU residents can import or export unlimited amounts of goods for personal use, on which duty has been paid, although guidelines for personal use are as follows: 800 cigarettes, 400 cigars or cigarillos, 1kg tobacco, 10 litres of spirits, 90 litres of wine, 110 litres of beer.

Non-EU nationals or EU citizens travelling from non-EU countries can import tax-free goods to the following limits: 200 cigarettes or 50 cigars or 100 cigarillos, or 250g of tobacco, 1 litre of spirits or 2 litres of fortified or sparkling wine, 4 litres of still wine, 16 litres of beer and other goods including gifts up to the value of €500.

Disabled travellers

Services for disabled people are better in The Netherlands than in most European countries. Museums and other public buildings usually have access for wheelchairs. Modern hotels will be fine but older hotels, especially in the tall historic canalside buildings, may not have lifts going up to higher floors.

The city itself is also tricky thanks to the traffic in places, the numerous canals with raised bridges, cobblestones, bollards and other minor hazards. Metro stations are equipped with lifts, but they may not always be easy to find. Trams and buses are difficult, train stations are generally good and there are special private wheelchair taxi services in the city such as Staxi (020-705 8888), though you will probably need to book ahead.

The Accessible Travel Netherlands website (www.accessibletravelnl.com), which is in both Dutch and English, will tell what the situation is in Amsterdam's public buildings.

Electricity

Voltage in Amsterdam and throughout the Netherlands is 220V, 50Hz, with plugs being the two round-pin continental type. If you need an adapter or a voltage trans-

former, buy one before leaving home as it will be hard to find one in Amsterdam.

Embassies and consulates

Although Amsterdam is the capital of the Netherlands, the diplomatic and political centre is in The Hague and all foreign embassies have their offices there.

Australia: Carnegielaan 4; tel: 070-310 8200; www.netherlands.embassy.gov.au.

Canada: Sophialaan 7; tel: 070-311 1600; www.canada.nl.

New Zealand: Eisenhowerlaan 77N; tel: 070-346 9324; www.mfat.govt.nz/netherlands

Republic of Ireland: Scheveningseweg 112; tel: 070-363 0993; www.irishembassy.nl.

South Africa: Wassenaarseweg 40; tel: 070-392 4501; www.zuidafrika.nl

UK: Lange Voorhout 10; tel: 070-427 0427; www.gov.uk/world/organisations/british-embassy-the-hague.

US: John Adams Park 1; tel: 070-310 2209; https://nl.usembassy.gov.

Consulates in Amsterdam

UK: Koningslaan 44; tel: 020-427 0427; www.gov.uk/world/organisations/british-consulate-general-amsterdam.

US: Museumplein 19; tel: 020-575 5330; https://nl.usembassy.gov/embassy-consulate/amsterdam.

Emergencies

For emergencies (fire, police or ambulance) dial 112. There are English-speaking operators, 24 hours a day.

Etiquette

When you're introduced to someone it's polite to shake their hand and say your name. You should also shake hands and say something polite when saying goodbye. If you've met someone before it's not necessary to do this, though you might in a business context. Only when you get to know someone well is it normal to greet them with a kiss on the cheek. Then it's three times, starting with the left cheek.

People tend to dress fairly casually (see page 110). If you're invited out for a meal the person inviting you will make it clear if they are going to host you and pay the bill. If nothing is said then assume you'll be splitting the bill – going Dutch, in other words. This also applies if a man and a woman are dining together. The Dutch believe in gender equality, so you will probably split the bill.

If someone knows you well then they may invite you to their home. If it's for a meal, take a bottle of wine. If it's just for a visit, then take flowers. Note that if you are invited for a meal then it's considered impolite to leave the table other than between courses, and also impolite to leave food on your plate.

Festivals and events

March

In honour of the 1345 Miracle of the Host, Catholics parade in the **Stille**

Koningsdag celebrations.

Omgang (Silent Procession), beginning at the Dam on the nearest Sun to the 15th.

Opening of the **Keukenhof** gardens at Lisse for the tulip season (Mar–May).

April

The **Bloemencorso** (Flower Parade) is an extravagant procession that begins in Aalsmeer and ends in Amsterdam, usually in the last week of April.

On Good Friday, the **Concertgebouw Orchestra** plays Bach's *The Passion According to Saint Matthew* in its concert hall.

National Museum Week (usually midmonth) features free or reduced-rate entry to most city museums.

Koningsdag (the King's official birthday) on the 27th (or the 26th if the 27th is a Sunday) is celebrated throughout the country. A street market and music festival bring Amsterdam to a standstill. Wear orange.

Kunst RAI (Arts RAI) at the RAI Exhibition centre (variable dates) showcases the art of a different country every year. www.kunstrai.nl

May

Bevrijdingsdag (Liberation Day) on 5 May celebrates the defeat of the Nazis. The activities in Amsterdam are comparable to those on Koningsdag.

June

The **Vondelpark**'s open-air theatre season runs June–Sept.

The **Holland Festival**, a month-long programme of music, theatre, opera, film and dance focuses on Amsterdam, The Hague, Rotterdam and Utrecht. www.hollandfestival.nl

The **Amsterdam Roots Festival** brings world music, dance, films, exhibitions and workshops to the Melkweg, on variable dates. www.amsterdamroots.nl

July

Gay Pride: exuberant festival in late July to early August culminating in a colourful boat parade on Prinsengracht.

August

The resort of Zandvoort has live jazz in its **Jazz Behind the Beach** festival, usually held in early August at various venues in the town.

The **Jordaan Festival**, a loosely structured series of musical and performance events, takes place in this Amsterdam district in the month's last days. www.jordaanfestival.nl

Grachtenfestival: a 10-day mid-month feast of classical music, with concerts held at venues along the canals. The highlight is the Prinsengracht Concert, on a pontoon moored outside the Pulitzer Hotel.

October

The **Amsterdam City Marathon** usually takes place in mid-October. www.tcsamsterdammarathon.nl

An apotheek.

November

On the Saturday nearest to the 17th November, the **Festival of Sint Nicolaas** is marked by a procession from Prins Hendrikkade to the city centre, featuring Nicolaas's helper, Zwarte Piet (Black Peter), with floats, bands and majorettes.

Amstelveen City Blues: this great blues festival takes place every November in the southern suburb of Amstelveen, usually on the last Saturday. International and local acts play at the Schouwburg Amstelveen theatre. www.amstelveencityblues.nl

December

Holiday on Ice at the RAI Exhibition Centre. www.rai.nl

H

Health

Medical facilities in Amsterdam are excellent. There are no health concerns, although mosquitoes can be a nuisance in the summer, so anti-mosquito sprays or creams are useful. You will not need inoculations and the water is safe to drink. Most doctors and other medical professionals speak English. Always take out suitable travel insurance to cover any health problem you may have on your trip. You will be asked to pay for some medical treatment and should cover yourself against something serious happening to you.

Emergency help

For 24-hour emergency medical and dental help, call the Central Medical Service: 020-592 3434. English-speaking operators can tell you which doctors and dentists are on duty, and which of them speak English (most of them do). Hotels and pharmacies can also advise.

There is an accident and emergency department at the Onze Lieve Vrouwe Gasthuis hospital, open 24-hours. 1e Oosterparkstraat 279, tel: 020-599 9111. (Note: this is well outside the city centre.)

EU citizens

If you are an EU citizen, you will be covered for medical treatment by participating doctors/hospitals if you have a European Health Insurance Card (EHIC), available online at www.ehic.org.uk. You will need to pay for treatment at the time but will be able to claim a refund on return.

Pharmacies

Many proprietary brands of drugs are available over the counter from any pharmacy (*apotheek*). A trained pharmacist will be able to give sound advice about medicines for minor ailments. These are normally open during usual shopping hours, roughly Mon–Fri 8.30am–5.30pm, and information about pharmacies open outside the hours is usually posted in pharmacy windows and given in the daily newspaper, *Het Parool*. Call 020-694 8709 to find out which pharmacies are open after hours and for referral to local doctors and dentists. The Leidsestraat Apotheek (Leidsestraat 74–6; tel: 020-422 0210) is open daily till 10pm.

Drag show at Lellebel.

Hours and holidays

Opening hours

Offices and most government offices are generally open Mon–Fri 9am–5pm. Banks are open Mon–Fri 9am–4pm, extended to 5pm for main branches; late opening Thu from 4.30pm–7pm. Shops are generally open Mon 10am or noon–6pm, Tue–Fri 9am–6pm, (until 9pm on Thu), Sat 9am–5pm. In the centre shops open Sun noon–5pm and some extend their opening hours in summer.

Public Holidays:

The following dates are official holidays:

1 January *Nieuwjaar* New Year's Day

27 April (or 26 if it falls on a Sunday) *Koningsdag* King's Birthday

25–26 December *Kerst* Christmas

Moveable holidays are as follows:

Goede Vrijdag Good Friday

Tweede Paasdag Easter Monday

Hemelvaartsdag Ascension Day

Tweede Pinksterdag Whit Monday

All shops and offices are closed for all the above holidays. Note that May 4 (Remembrance Day) and May 5 (Liberation Day) are not official public holidays but many businesses do close on those days.

Internet facilities

Many city hotels, along with some cafés, bars, coffee houses and other locations offer usually free or sometimes paid-for Wi-Fi internet access, with hotels often providing terminals for guest use. This has made the dedicated cybercafé virtually superfluous and you will struggle to find one in the city centre.

L

Language

All Dutch children learn English in school and most people you meet while visiting Amsterdam will speak English fluently. The Dutch attitude is the pragmatic one: we have to learn other languages as who's going to speak Dutch?

Eavesdropping on any Dutch conversation, you could be forgiven for thinking that Dutch people constantly need to clear their throat! This Germanic language regularly uses a guttural consonant similar to the 'ch' in the Scottish word 'loch'. In Dutch terms this is known as the 'soft g', although the 'hard g' sounds almost the same – if you look at Dutch words that begin with a 'g', then you can reasonably assume the word starts with that infamous 'ch'.

LGBTQ Travellers

Amsterdam is an extremely friendly city for gay and lesbian visitors. Gay Pride in late July/early August is one of the world's largest gay celebrations, drawing over 350,000 participants. There are hotels that cater specifically for gay customers and a vibrant social scene.

A novel form of transport.

The website of the Gay Tourist Information Centre (GAYtic) at Spuistraat 44 (tel: 020-330 1461) is packed with useful information, as is www.nighttours.com, a travel guide to the city's gay life. Reguliersdwarsstraat is the city's most prominent gay street.

M

Media

Print media
Many English newspapers and magazines can be readily bought in the city. British daily papers are available soon after they are on sale at home. US papers will be a day old.

Radio
The BBC can be picked up with good reception on long wave, and the BBC World Service and the Voice of America are both available.

Television
There are a number of Dutch television stations mainly serving the local community and sometimes taking services from various European countries, including British stations. The Dutch use subtitles to translate foreign programmes, rather than dubbing, so you will be able to understand the broadcasts – this is one of the reasons why the Dutch are so adept at speaking English and other languages. Most major hotels offer CNN and the BBC in your room.

English-language publications
Several tourist information magazines in English are available, either for a charge at newsstands or free at many hotels. The best is *I amsterdam Magazine*, published by the tourist board every three months and providing lively sections on what to do and see in the city.

Money

Currency
In common with most other EU countries, the euro (€) is used in the Netherlands. Notes are denominated in 5, 10, 20, 50, 100, 200 and 500 euros; coins in 1 and 2 euros and 1, 2, 5, 10, 20 and 50 cents.

Credit cards
All major credit cards are accepted, though not as widely as in some cities. Some shops and restaurants still prefer cash, and some of the less expensive hotels

Cash machines
International ATMs are widespread and are indicated by the Cirrus or Plus signs on the machine.

Tipping
Service charges are included in all bar, restaurant and hotel bills. However, an extra tip to show gratitude for good service is always appreciated. It is appropriate to leave the small change on the table in bars and cafés. The following situations are still discretionary:

Taxi fares: round up the fare.
Hotel porter: €1–2 per bag.

Albert Cuyp Market.

Tour guide: 10–15 percent.
Concierge: discretionary according to services provided.

P

Post

The Dutch postal service is operated by the private PostNL company, which also operates in several other European countries. Larger post offices are slowly disappearing, being replaced by small branches inside supermarkets, bookshops, tobacco and other shops. You can find the nearest outlet by going to the PostNL website (www.postnl.nl) and entering the local postcode.

Amsterdam now only has its main post office, located at Singel 250 and open Mon–Fri 8am–6pm, Sat 9am–5pm.

The cost of sending a postcard or letter up to 20gms to either the UK or USA is €1.40. Post boxes are orange.

R

Religion

The Netherlands is predominantly Calvinist, with the Dutch Reformed Church being the most popular denomination. There is a substantial Roman Catholic minority (or majority in the south). But if you visit any church in Amsterdam during a Sunday service you will find that, as in many places, more people claim to be religious than actually attend church.

S

Smoking

Smoking is prohibited in many places in Amsterdam including: public transport, in offices, in public areas including shopping malls, airports, stations and public places, in hotels and restaurants, and, confusingly, in the coffeeshops where they are permitted to sell soft drugs, unless a separate tobacco smoking area is provided. In 2018, the Dutch Court of Appeal banned separate smoking rooms in bars, pubs, clubs and restaurants.

T

Telephones

The international code for the Netherlands is 31, and the city code for Amsterdam is 020. To call a number within the city use just the seven-digit number. To call an Amsterdam number from other parts of the Netherlands, dial 020 first. If dialling from outside the country dial your international country code + 31 20 and the seven-digit number.

Virtually all of the public phones around the city are out of use. If you happen to find one that is working you will need a credit card or a phonecard, available from newsagents and tobacconists.

Roaming is possible on Holland's tri-band and quad-band enabled GSM mobile-phone network. Phones to rent and purchase are widely available from phone stores, as are prepaid SIM cards

Centraal Station.

for using your own (unlocked) phone at Dutch rates. Be sure to bring an appropriate plug adaptor and, if needed, a voltage transformer for charging your phone. For citizens of 31 European Economic Area countries, currently including the UK and Ireland, roaming charges were abolished in mid-2017 yet under a fair use policy some restrictions on the free use of mobile phones are still in place. What will happen after the UK leaves the EU in March 2019 is currently unclear.

International dialling codes:
To make an international call dial 00 followed by the country code:
Australia +61
Canada +1
Ireland +353
UK +44
US +1

Time zones

The Netherlands is one hour ahead of Greenwich Mean Time (GMT). From the last weekend in March to the last weekend in October, the clocks are advanced one hour, and this change corresponds with the rest of the EU. During the European summer, this means that when it is noon in Amsterdam it will be 11am in London and 6am in New York.

Tourist information

For information, maps, hotel bookings and tickets, visit the VVV tourist office (tel: 020-702 600; www.iamsterdam.com) at Stationsplein 10, opposite the entrance to Centraal Station, daily 9am–5pm. Take a ticket when you arrive and expect a long wait, though the level of service provided is excellent.

Staff can arrange hotel accommodation (for a small fee), book theatre and museum tickets, sell you the I amsterdam City Card and provide a city map (for a small charge). There is also an I amsterdam store and visitor centre inside Centraal Station (Mon–Wed 8am–7pm, Thu–Sat 8am–8pm, Sun 10am–6pm) and a visitor centre at Schiphol Airport (daily 7am–10pm).

Transport

Arrival by air
Amsterdam Schiphol Airport (AMS; www.schiphol.nl), 18km (11 miles) southwest of the city centre, is one of the busiest and most modern airports in Europe. It acts as a gateway to Europe for airlines from around the world. Its tax-free shopping centre is considered among the best in the world.

From the UK there are direct flights from all the London airports on KLM, British Airways, easyJet, CityJet and FlyBe. There are also flights from Edinburgh, Glasgow, Manchester and many other UK cities. From the USA, Delta flies to Amsterdam from many US cities, as does United and KLM. United and KLM also fly to Amsterdam from Canada. There are no direct flights to Amsterdam from Australia or New Zealand. You would need to

Public toilets can be hard to come by in the city.

change in London, Paris or another European city.

There is a good rail connection from Schiphol Airport to Amsterdam Centraal Station. Trains run 24 hours a day: every 4–10 minutes from 6am–midnight, and less frequent from midnight–6am. The journey takes 15–20 minutes and costs €4.30. Tickets can be bought from machines with clear instructions in English and can be paid for with cash or credit card.

Every 10–30 minutes from 6.30am–9pm a Connexxion Hotel Shuttle bus (tel: 088-339 4741; www.schipholho telshuttle.nl) leaves the airport, stopping at many of the major hotels. Tickets (€17) are sold at the Connexxion counter in the arrivals hall and on the bus. The bus will also take you back to the airport (return ticket costs €28).

If you are staying near Museumplein or Leidseplein, it is far cheaper to take bus No. 397 (marked Amsterdam Airport Express), which takes 25 minutes and departs every 7–30 minutes between 5.26am and 12.46am, and costs €6 single/€10 return.

A taxi from the airport to the centre costs around €40–60, depending on which part of the city you're going to.

Arrival by train

In 2018 Eurostar (tel: 03432-186 186; www.eurostar.com), in cooperation with Dutch Railways, launched a direct service between London and Amsterdam. The journey time is 3 hours 41 minutes. As of September 2018, there isn't yet a direct return train from Amsterdam to London available. The quickest route is via Brussels Zuid/Midi (4 hours 45 minutes).

Centraal Station stands on the harbour and faces into the city, with many places easily reached on foot or by tram or metro. There's a tourist office both inside and outside the station to offer help, and the station is the city's main transport hub for metro and tram lines.

Arrival by sea

P&O Ferries operates a daily service from Hull to Rotterdam (tel: 0800-130 0030; www.poferries.com), from where there are train connections to Amsterdam. Stena Line (tel: 0844-770 7070; www.stena-line.co.uk) sails from Harwich to Hoek van Holland, from where you would need to take a train into Rotterdam and then on to Amsterdam. DFDS Seaways (tel: 0871-522 9955; www.dfdsseaways.co.uk) from Newcastle to IJmuiden near Amsterdam, with train connections into the city.

Public transport

Public transport in Amsterdam is excellent. The GVB (tel: 0900-8011; www.gvb.nl) municipal transport company runs a comprehensive network of trams, buses, trains, metro and boats. The ferries are free. Information, route maps, timetables and public transport passes are available from the GVB Tickets & Info office on Stationsplein, outside Centraal Station.

OV-chipkaart. In Amsterdam and throughout the Netherlands, journeys for

Cycling in Vondelpark.

the trams, buses and metro are paid for with a public transport card, the credit card-size OV-chipkaart. 'OV' stands for Openbaar Vervoer (public transport). The most convenient option for visitors are the one-hour cards or (multi-) day cards available from the conductor on buses and trams, at GVB ticket vending machines or information locations, or an anonymous card that can be purchased or topped up with credit at newsstands and supermarkets as well as GVB ticket vending machines and information offices.

Tram: Amsterdam has an excellent network of trams. Don't forget to either buy your ticket when you board or register your travel pass or travel card on the machine. Many tram stops are in the middle of the road, with traffic passing on both sides so take care when getting on and off, and keep young children close to you. If a tram has a conductor you must enter at or towards the rear, otherwise enter by any door. Press one of the bells found at regular intervals along the carriage to get off at the next stop.

Bus: An extensive bus network operated by the GVB, and by regional operators like Connexxion (www.connexxion.nl) and Arriva (www.arriva.nl), go to places the trams might not reach, but the tram network is generally the best way for visitors to get around. After midnight when trams stop, a night bus network is in operation.

Metro: The Amsterdam metro currently has five lines designed to link the city centre with the suburbs and as such

are not as useful as other forms of public transport for visiting tourist attractions. A controversial new line linked the south of the city with the north in mid-2018. The tunnel runs under the historic centre and major delays have been caused by damage to the foundations of several historic buildings and spiralling costs.

Ferries: Ferry GVB ferries transport passengers (and their bikes and mopeds) from Centraal Station across the River IJ free of charge.

Taxis: Amsterdam's black or orange-coloured taxis can be found at ranks across the city, including Centraal Station, the Dam, Rembrandtplein and Leidseplein. Officially you are not allowed to flag them down in the street but it is always worth a try. Note that they are legally obligated to provide you with a receipt at the end of your journey, which gives full information about your trip. If you have a complaint you can contact www.taxiklacht.nl or call 0900-202 1881 (Mon–Fri 9am–5pm).

Generally taxis are not the most economic or quickest way to get around within the city itself. Public transport or foot is usually better, but late at night or if journeying to or from the suburbs, a taxi is useful. The maximum start price for a journey is €2.95, and the maximum price per minute is €0.36.

Amsterdam's main taxi company is Taxi Centrale (tel: 020-777 7777). Others include Aemstel Taxi (0297 330033), My Taxi Centrale (020-475 0320), STA (020-354 2232) and Staxi (020-705 8888).

Amsterdam has an excellent tram network.

Driving

Driving within Amsterdam is not recommended. Streetside and canalside parking is expensive and difficult to find, and the excellent transport system precludes the need for your own car. There are very reasonably-priced Park & Ride parking lots off the A10 ring road, where you can leave your car for a maximum of four days.

Vehicles are driven on the right. At roundabouts, give way to traffic from the right (unless signs indicate otherwise).

The Netherlands has very strict drink-driving laws and it is safest to assume you shouldn't even have one drink if you're planning to drive. The legal limit is 220 micrograms per litre of exhaled breath or 0.5 grams of alcohol per litre of blood. Police may hand out an on-the-spot fine, and your car may be confiscated.

In towns or built up areas: 30 or 50kph (20 or 30mph). On dual carriageways and other motorways: 120kph (75mph) reduced to 100kph (62mph) in wet weather, 80kph (50mph) on regional roads. Other limits may be posted.

If you travel to Holland in your own car, you will need to carry your driving licence, registration document, or document of ownership, valid insurance, a red warning triangle and an international country identification sticker on the back of the car.

If you need help, the ANWB (Dutch Automobile Association; tel: 088-269 2222; www.anwb.nl) offers roadside assistance. If you hire a car, make sure you know what to do if you break down.

Car hire. The major international car rental companies all have desks ate Schiphol Airport and most have offices in the city centre too. These include:

Avis: Nassaukade 380, tel: 088-284 7020.

Europcar: Overtoom 197, tel: 020-683 2123.

Hertz: Overtoom 333, tel: 020-612 2441.

Visas and passports

Citizens of the EU, US, Canada, Australia and New Zealand do not need a visa and can visit for up to three months with a valid passport. Your passport only needs to be valid for the proposed length of your stay in Amsterdam.

Weights and measures

The Netherlands uses the metric system.

Women travellers

Women in The Netherlands have equal rights and it is generally safe for women to travel alone. You only need worry about the usual things that affect everyone in a big city: see Crime and safety (page 111). Dutch men are, in general, very polite towards women but any unwelcome approaches should be met with a firm but friendly response. If you do get hassled, most people would come straight to your aid.

A scene from Amsterdamned.

BOOKS AND FILM

The rich setting and unique lifestyle in Amsterdam have inspired writers to use it as a backdrop for fiction, especially crime fiction and its history as a city has also produced some fine non-fiction books about the Dutch capital. One of the most-read books of all-time, *The Diary of Anne Frank*, is just one title that would be good background reading when preparing a visit. The fact that many artists, not least Rembrandt, have lived here means there are also many books on the history of art and the lives of the artists.

There have been films made about the life of Rembrandt too, but surprisingly, despite its visual appeal, Amsterdam hasn't quite attracted the same number of film-makers as cities like, say, Venice or Paris. Perhaps the difficulty of filming in its busy narrow streets, and the difficulty of hauling equipment in and out, partly account for that.

Books

Non-fiction

The best chronicler of the city in recent years has been the journalist Geert Mak, and nothing beats his **Amsterdam: A Brief Life of the City** by way of preparing for a visit. It is anything but brief, though never less than fascinating.

Anne Frank's **The Diary of a Young Girl** is also top of the list for required reading, preferably before you visit the house in which she wrote her diary while she and her family hid from the Nazis during World War II.

Crime fiction

Amsterdam has inspired several crime writers. You can relax with the Van der Valk cop novels of Nicolas Freeling, and Janwillem van de Wetering has written an excellent series of books under the umbrella title of Amsterdam Cops, the first being **Outsider in Amsterdam**. The Inspector Dekok mysteries by A.C. Baantjer are also good, easy reads and very atmospheric. Award-winning crime writer David Hewson also uses Amsterdam as the setting for his Pieter Vos detective series, beginning with **The House of Dolls**.

Fiction

Given the appetite of Amsterdam's inhabitants for culture and debate, it's perhaps surprising that so few of its authors are widely read outside the Netherlands. The 'Great Three' of Dutch post-war literature – Willem Hermans, Harry Mulisch and Gerard Reve – are undoubtedly worthy of greater attention from translators and publishers.

The prolific Harry Mulisch, whose novel **The Discovery of Heaven** was voted 'best Dutch-language book ever' by Dutch readers, is probably the one whose works you're most likely to find

translated into other languages. Look for his novel **Last Call**, which tells the story of a Dutch actor in Amsterdam.

The novelist and journalist Cees Noteboom, who has won many literary awards, has also had several of his works translated. His novel **Rituals** evokes the mood of Amsterdam as his protagonist walks the city streets.

Ian McEwan's novel **Amsterdam** won the 1998 Booker Prize and although only the final scenes of the book take place in Amsterdam, it's a powerful read about two friends who make a euthanasia pact.

If you're planning on visiting Rembrandt's House then Sylvie Matton's novel **Rembrandt's Whore** is a must-read, depicting as it does the reality of the artist's life there including his descent into penury, a feature of his life often overshadowed by his posthumous great fame.

The Coffee Trader by David Liss is a fictionalised account of life in Amsterdam beginning in 1659 when it was one of the world's most exciting and important cities, home to the world's first stock exchange. **Tulip Fever** by Deborah Moggach, who wrote **The Last Marigold Hotel**, is also a fictionalised recreation of 17th-century Amsterdam when tulip fever was at its height and life in the city was buzzing and dramatic.

The Book of Revelation by Rupert Thomson is set in Amsterdam and tells the haunting story of a male dancer who leaves his house one day to go shopping and finds himself abducted. It's full of little glimpses into life in the city.

Film

The life of artists has always appealed to film-makers, from Kirk Douglas as Vincent van Gogh to the 2003 movie **Girl with a Pearl Earring**, inspired by the famous painting by Vermeer. Although Vermeer lived in Delft, where he painted the work, much of the film was actually shot in Amsterdam.

The life of Rembrandt inspired a 1936 movie, produced and directed by Alexander Korda and with the artist played by Charles Laughton. Peter Greenaway's 2007 movie **Nightwatching** was also about Rembrandt, focussing on him working on his most famous painting, **The Night Watch**, and with English actor Martin Freeman as Rembrandt.

Amsterdam's 'Skinny Bridge' makes an appearance near the beginning of the James Bond movie, **Diamonds are Forever**, with Bond posing as a diamond smuggler. The 1971 thriller **Puppet on a Chain**, from the book by Alastair MacLean, features Amsterdam rather more prominently with a chase sequence along the canals. The darker side of Amsterdam's movie location potential is made good use of in the 1988 Dutch horror movie, **Amsterdammed**, when a serial killer uses the canals at night to get around and murder his victims. You'll also spot Amsterdam in the 1974 Wim Wenders film, **Alice in the Cities**.

The latest film shot in Amsterdam is **The Dinner** (2017) directed by Oren Moverman, based on Herman Koch's novel, starring Richard Gere and Laura Linney.

ABOUT THIS BOOK

This *Explore Guide* has been produced by the editors of Insight Guides, whose books have set the standard for visual travel guides since 1970. With top-quality photography and authoritative recommendations, these guidebooks bring you the very best routes and itineraries in the world's most exciting destinations.

BEST ROUTES

The routes in the book provide something to suit all budgets, tastes and trip lengths. As well as covering the destination's many classic attractions, the itineraries track lesser-known sights, and there are also excursions for those who want to extend their visit outside the city. The routes embrace a range of interests, so whether you are an art fan, a gourmet, a history buff or have kids to entertain, you will find an option to suit.

We recommend reading the whole of a route before setting out. This should help you to familiarise yourself with it and enable you to plan where to stop for refreshments – options are shown in the 'Food and Drink' box at the end of each tour.

For our pick of the tours by theme, consult Recommended Routes for… (see pages 6–7).

INTRODUCTION

The routes are set in context by this introductory section, giving an overview of the destination to set the scene, plus background information on food and drink, shopping and more, while a succinct history timeline highlights the key events over the centuries.

DIRECTORY

Also supporting the routes is a Directory chapter, with a clearly organised A–Z of practical information, our pick of where to stay while you are there and select restaurant listings; these eateries complement the more low-key cafés and restaurants that feature within the routes and are intended to offer a wider choice for evening dining. Also included here are some nightlife listings and our recommendations for books and films about the destination.

ABOUT THE AUTHORS

Mike Gerrard is an award-winning travel writer who has visited Amsterdam many times, and look forward to visiting it many more times. He has written several guides to the city along with travel pieces for newspapers, magazines and websites. This book builds on content written by George McDonald. This new edition was thoroughly updated by Magdalena Stadnik-Helsztyńska.

CONTACT THE EDITORS

We hope you find this Explore Guide useful, interesting and a pleasure to read. If you have any questions or feedback on the text, pictures or maps, please do let us know. If you have noticed any errors or outdated facts, or have suggestions for places to include on the routes, we would be delighted to hear from you. Please drop us an email at hello@insightguides.com. Thanks!

CREDITS

Explore Amsterdam
Editor: Tom Fleming
Authors: Mike Gerrard, George McDonald
Head of DTP and Pre-Press: Daniel May
Update Production: Apa Digital
Picture Editor: Tom Smyth
Cartography: Carte
Photo credits: Alamy 52, 84, 122; Allard Bovenberg/AFF/AFHí 29L; Getty Images 1, 8/9T, 22, 23, 24/25T, 55, 57T, 59, 60/61, 73, 74T, 79, 90/91T; Greg Gladman/Apa Publications 4ML, 4MC, 4MR, 4MR, 4MC, 4ML, 6ML, 6BC, 7T, 7MR, 7M, 8ML, 8MC, 8ML, 8MC, 8MR, 8MR, 12, 13, 14, 14/15, 15L, 17, 19L, 20, 21, 24ML, 24MC, 24MR, 24ML, 24MC, 24MR, 26/27, 28/29, 30T, 30B, 30/31, 31L, 32, 33, 34, 34/35, 35L, 36, 38/39, 42, 43, 44, 45L, 46, 46/47, 47L, 48, 49, 50, 50/51, 51L, 52/53, 57B, 58, 62, 63, 64, 64/65, 65L, 70, 71L, 72T, 72B, 74B, 75, 76/77T, 76B, 90ML, 90MC, 90MR, 90MC, 90ML, 100, 100/101, 102, 103, 108, 109, 110, 111, 114, 115, 116, 117, 118, 119, 120; iStock 6MC, 10/11, 18/19, 53L, 66/67T, 78, 80, 81L, 83, 86; JL Marshall/Rijksmuseum 37, 41; Leonardo 90MR, 92, 93, 94, 94/95, 95L, 96, 96/97, 97L, 98, 99, 104, 104/105, 105L, 106, 107; NBTC 6TL, 16, 18, 39L, 66B, 68, 69, 70/71, 80/81, 82, 87, 101L, 112, 113; Public domain 38; Shutterstock 4/5T, 7MR, 28, 44/45, 54, 56, 85, 88/89, 121; The Kobal Collection 123; Vincent van Gogh Foundation 40
Cover credits: Getty Images (main) iStock (bottom)

Printed by CTPS – China

Second Edition 2019

DISTRIBUTION

UK, Ireland and Europe
Apa Publications (UK) Ltd
sales@insightguides.com
United States and Canada
Ingram Publisher Services
ips@ingramcontent.com
Australia and New Zealand
Woodslane
info@woodslane.com.au
Southeast Asia
Apa Publications (Singapore) Pte
singaporeoffice@insightguides.com
Worldwide
Apa Publications (UK) Ltd
sales@insightguides.com

SPECIAL SALES, CONTENT LICENSING AND COPUBLISHING

Insight Guides can be purchased in bulk quantities at discounted prices. We can create special editions, personalised jackets and corporate imprints tailored to your needs.
sales@insightguides.com
www.insightguides.biz

INDEX

A

accommodation **92**
Adelaarswegveer **83**
age restrictions **110**
American Book Center **34**
Amsteldijk **58**
Amstel, River **31**
Amstel Station **56, 59**
Amstelveenseweg **66**
Amsterdam American Hotel **53, 54, 60**
Amsterdam Museum **34**
Amsterdamse Bos (Amsterdam Wood) **66**
Amsterdamse Waterleidingduinen **82**
Andrieshofje **62**
Anne Frank Huis **27**
Archaeological Museum **81**
Artis Royal Zoo **48**
   Aquarium **48**
   Geological Museum **48**
   Planetarium **48**
Athenaeum Illustre **44**
Athenaeum News Centre **34**

B

Bakenesserkerk **80**
Bayside Beach Club **73**
beach, the **82**
beer **18**
Begijnhof **34, 80**
Bellevue Theater **53**
Berlage Brug **58**
Beurs van Berlage **43**
Bijenkorf **32**
Binnenhaven **85**
Bird Market **27**
Blauwbrug **58**
Blauwe Engel (Blue Angel) **56**
Bloemenmarkt (Flower Market) **28**
Blue Gold Fish **28**
books **122**

Bourbon Street **71**
Brouwersgracht **61**
budgeting **110**
Buiksloterweg **50**
Bulldog Palace **69**

C

canals **26**
Casa Rosso **77**
Centraal Station **49, 54**
children **110**
Circuit Park Zandvoort **82**
Claes Claesz Hofje **62**
climate **14, 110**
clogs **85**
clothing **110**
Cobra Museum **56**
Concertgebouw **39, 56, 81**
Coster Diamonds **56**
crime and safety **111**
customs **111**

D

Dam, the **32, 75**
De la Mar Theater **53**
De Waag **45**
Diary of a Young Girl, the **122**
disabled travellers **111**
Duivel **74**
Durgerdam **84**

E

economy **14**
Edam **85**
eetcafés **17**
electricity **112**
embassies and consulates **112**
emergencies **112**
Erotic Museum **45**
Eteresheim **85**
etiquette **112**

F

Farmers' Market **27**
festivals and events **113**

film **123**
flea market **63**
food and drink **16**
Frans Hals Museum – Hof **81**

G

gay/lesbian travellers **116**
geography **10**
Grand hotel, the **44**
Grote Markt **81**
Grote Vijver **68**

H

Haarlem **78**
Haarlem Station **78**
Hague **86**
   Beelden aan Zee **89**
   Binnenhof **88**
   Buitenhof **88**
   De Resident **87**
   Hof Vijver lake **88**
   Kurhaus **89**
   Madurodam Miniature City **89**
   Mauritshuis art museum **87**
   New Babylon **86**
   Oude Stadhuis **88**
   Paleis Noordeinde **88**
   Panorama Mesdag **88**
   Plein **87**
   Ridderzaal **88**
   Scheveningen **89**
   Sea Life Scheveningen **89**
   Vredespaleis **88**
Hash Marihuana and Hemp Museum **45**
health **114**
Heeren van Aemstel **74**
Herengracht **27**
Het Houten Huys **35**
history **11, 22**
Hofje van Oorschot **82**
Holland Casino Amsterdam **56, 70**

Holland Casino Zandvoort 82
Homomonument 28
Hoorn 85
Hortus Botanicus (Botanical Garden) 46
  Butterfly House 47
  Palm House 47
  Semicircle 47
  Three-Climate House 47
hours and holidays 115
Huys-Zitten-Weduwe-Hofje 62

I

IJsselmeer lake 83
internet facilities 115

J

Jazz Café Alto 71
jenever (genever) 19
Jewish Quarter (Jodenbuurt) 63
Jewish Resistance Fighters' Memorial 65
Joods Historisch Museum 64
Jordaan, the 60

K

Karthuizerplantsoen 61
Kattenkabinet (Cat Museum) 30
Keizersgracht 54
Keizersgracht bridge 27
Kindermuseum 48
Kleine Gartmanplantsoen 70
Kleine Komedie 73
Kleine Lijnbaansgracht 35
Koninklijk Paleis 32
Korte Golf 74

L

La Margarita 74
language 115

Leidseplein 35, 69
Leidsestraat 54
local customs 14

M

Mac Bike 57
Madame Tussauds 34
Magere Brug 58, 59
Magna Plaza 54
Maloe Melo 71
Marken 84
Market Square 27
Martin Luther King Park 58
Max Euweplein 70
media 116
Melkweg 70
money 116
Monnickendam 84
Mozes en Aäronkerk 65
Müller organ 81
Mulligan's Irish Music Bar 73
Muntplein 30, 72
Munttoren 30
Museum Het Rembrandthuis 65
Museumplein 38, 56
Museum Quarter 37
Museum van Loon 30

N

Nationaal Monument 32
Nationale Opera en Ballet 73
Negen Straatjes (Nine Little Streets) 28
NEMO Science Centre 51
Nieuwe Kerk 33
Nieuwe Meer 68
Nieuwmarkt 45
Night Watch, the 38
Noorderkerk 27, 60
Noordermarkt 27

O

Oost-Indisch Huis 45
Openluchttheater 68

Opera 64
Oude Hoogstraat 45
Oude Kerk 44, 76
Ouderkerk aan de Amstel 59
Oudezijds Voorburgwal 44, 76

P

Paradiso 71
Pathé City 70
Pathé Tuschinski cinema 73
pier 50
Pieter Cornelisz Hooftstraat 41, 56
Plantage district 46
politics 14
population 14
Portuguese Synagogue 64
post 117
Prinsengracht 52, 54, 62
Prinsenhof 44
Purmerend 85

R

RAI Amsterdam Convention Centre 56
religion 117
Rembrandtplein 35, 73
Rijksmuseum 37, 56
Roeibaan 68
Rokin 35
Rosse Buurt 80
Royal Theater 58

S

Scheepvaart Museum 51
Sex Palace 77
shopping 20
side-canals 52
Sint-Bavokerk 81
Skinny Sisters 59
smoking 117
Spaarne, River 80
Spiegelgracht 53
Spiegelkwartier 35
Spui 34

Stadharts Shopping Centre 56
Stadhuis 64, 81
Stadsschouwburg (City Theatre) 54, 70
Stedelijk Museum 40, 56
Stromma 52

T

't Aepjen 45
Tasmanstraat 51
telephones 118
Teylers Museum 80
Thorbeckeplein Art Market 35
time zones 118
't Lieverdje (Little Darling) 34
toilets 118
tourist information 118

tours and guides 119
transport 119
  air transport 119
  public transport 120
  sea transport 120
  train transport 120
transportdriving 121
Tropenmuseum 48
Tuschinski Theater 35

U

Utrechtse Brug 59

V

Van Gogh Museum 41, 56
Vleeshal 81
Volendam 84
Vondelpark 41

Vrije Universiteit 56
Vrij Universiteit Hospital 67
Vroom & Dreesmann 56

W

Waag 80
Waalse Kerk 80
Warder 85
Waterlooplein 63
Westerkerk 28, 62
Westermarkt 28
WilletHolthuysen Museum 30
Woltheus Cruises 80
World Trade Center Amsterdam 56

Z

Zandvoort 82

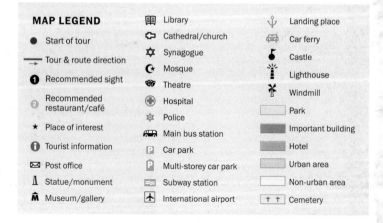

MAP LEGEND

- ● Start of tour
- → Tour & route direction
- ❶ Recommended sight
- ❷ Recommended restaurant/café
- ★ Place of interest
- ❶ Tourist information
- ✉ Post office
- ⚏ Statue/monument
- Ṁ Museum/gallery

- 📖 Library
- ✝ Cathedral/church
- ✡ Synagogue
- ☪ Mosque
- 🎭 Theatre
- ✚ Hospital
- ✿ Police
- 🚌 Main bus station
- P Car park
- P Multi-storey car park
- 🚇 Subway station
- ✈ International airport

- ⚓ Landing place
- 🚗 Car ferry
- Castle
- Lighthouse
- Windmill
- Park
- Important building
- Hotel
- Urban area
- Non-urban area
- † † Cemetery